EARTH AND SPACE

DR MIKE GOLDSMITH,
MARGARET HYNES AND BARBARA TAYLOR

KINGFISHER

First published 2016 by Kingfisher
an imprint of Macmillan Children's Books
20 New Wharf Road, London N1 9RR
Associated companies throughout the world
www.panmacmillan.com

Copyright © Macmillan Publishers International Ltd 2016

ISBN 978-0-7534-3944-9

Consultant: Dr Rob Francis, King's College London

Illustrations by: Chris Moore, Alex Pang, The Peter Bull Art Studio

9 8 7 6 5 4 3 2 1
1TR/0216/UTD/WKT/128MA

A CIP catalogue record for this book is available from the British Library.

Printed in China

Note to readers: The website addresses listed in this book are correct at the time of publishing.
However, due to the ever-changing nature of the internet, website addresses and content can change.
Websites can contain links that are unsuitable for children. The publisher cannot be held responsible for
changes in website addresses or content, or for information obtained through third-party websites.
We strongly advise that internet searches should be supervised by an adult.

INVESTIGATE ICONS:

 Book to read

 Place to visit

 Website to visit

The Publisher would like to thank the following for permission to reproduce their material. Every care has been taken to trace copyright holders.
(t = top, b = bottom, c = centre, r = right, l = left):
Front Cover tl Shutterstock/Matt Tilghman, tcl Shutterstock/Tatjana Romanova; tc Shutterstock/Noradoa; tr Shutterstock/Willyam Bradberry; c NASA; back cover bl iStock/m-gucci; bc iStock/MarcelC; cr iStock/3Dsculptor; page 1, 18tl, 32cl Dreamstime/Alexander Evstigneev; 3–4 iStock/fotoVoyager; 5 Dreamstime/Forplayday; 6–7 Science Photo Library (SPL)/Detlev van Ravenswaay; 6c Shutterstock/GK; 6r SPL/M–SAT Ltd; 10 Corbis/Andy Rain/epa; 11 Corbis/Lloyd Cluff; 12 PA/AP; 13tl Corbis/Daniel Basualto; 15t Getty/OSF/John Downer; 15b Corbis/Torleif Svensson; 16–17 Getty/Panoramic Images; 16cr Getty/Digital Vision; 17bl Corbis/Guenter Rossenbach; 17box Shutterstock/Bryan Brazil; 17boxt Shutterstock/Invisible; 17boxtc Shutterstock/Wallenrock; 17boxc Shutterstock/Keith Levit; 17boxbl Shutterstock/Manamana; 17boxbr Getty/National Geographic Society (NGS); 17bc Getty/Visuals Unlimited; 17bcl Getty/Visuals Unlimited; 17br Alamy; 18cl Dreamstime/Jiri Vaclavek; 18bl iStock/Macsnap; 18tr Dreamstime/Vulkanette; 18br iStock/Robert_Ford; 19 iStock/Michael Cunliffe; 20tl Getty/Allan White; 20bl Getty/Ted Mead; 20cr Superstock/Charles Marden Fitch; 20br Corbis/Theo Allofs; 21c Science Photo Library (SPL)/Martin Jakobsson; 21cr Corbis/NASA; 21bc Getty/Allan White; 22tr Alamy/Idris Ahmed; 23bl SPL/Eye of Science; 25c SPL/NOAA PMEL Vents Program; 25br SPL/Dr Ken Macdonald; 26–27 Corbis/Theo Allofs; 26cl Shutterstock/ANP; 26bl Getty/DAJ; 27bl NAS; 28–29 Frank Lane Picture Agency (FLPA)/Minden/Hedgehog House; 28cr Corbis/Danny Lehman; 28br Shutterstock/JayZee; 29tl Alamy/Jupiter Images; 29br Alamy/StockShot; 30bl Corbis/ NASA; 30br SPL/Alfred Pasieka; 31tl SPL/Kenneth Libbrecht; 32tl iStock/olof van der steen; 32bl iStock/NCHANT; 32tr Dreamstime/Steve Allen; 32br Dreamstime/Insider2d; 33 iStock/Khlongwangchao; 34–35 Corbis/Frans Lemmens/epa; 34l Shutterstock/Sasha Buzko; 34c Woodfall/ Photoshot; 34r Corbis/Jose Fuste Raga; 35c Naturepl/David Shale; 35r Naturepl/Martin Gabriel; 36–37 Naturepl/Anup Shah; 36c Getty/Richard Du Toit/Minden; 36br Alamy/blickwinkel; 37c Shutterstock/Lindsay Basson; 37bl Corbis/Axiom/Toby Adamson; 37br Corbis/Frans Lanting; 38 Getty/OSF; 38tl Shutterstock/Sara Berdon; 38tc Alamy/Amazon Images; 38tr Corbis/Kevin Schafer; 38c Shutterstock/Elena Mirage; 38cr FLPA/Minden; 38br Naturepl/Pete Oxford; 39 Naturepl/Doug Wechsler; 39boxc Getty/Radius Images; 39boxr Getty/Riser; 39bc Photoshot/ NHPA/James Carmichael Jr; 39br Alamy/Norman Owen Tomalin; 40tl FLPA/Kevin Schafer; 40cl Ardea/Thomas Marent; 40tr Shutterstock/Rob Jenner; 40bl FLPA/Michael&Patricia Fogden/Minden; 40br Nature/Shatti & Rozinski; 41tl FLPA/David Hosking; 41tr FLPA/Cyril Russo/Minden; 41bl Alamy/Robert Harding; 41cr FLPA/Cyril Russo/Minden; 42–43 Corbis/DLILL; 42br Getty/Norbert Rosing; 42cl Shutterstock/Serg Zastavkin; 43tr Shutterstock/Bildagentur Zoonar GmbH; 43cr Shutterstock/Erni; 43b Corbis/Minden Pictures; 44l Naturepl/Doug Perrine; 44tr SeaPics/James D. Watt; 44br SeaPics/Masa Ushioda; 44–45 Getty/Norbert Wu/Minden; 45tc Naturepl/David Shale; 45bl SeaPics/Nat Sumanatemeya; 45tr SeaPics/David Schrichte; 45cr Image Quest Marine/Peter Batson; 45br SPL/NOAA; 46tl Dreamstime/Outdoorsman; 46cl Dreamstime/Vilainecrevette; 46bl Dreamstime; 46tr Dreamstime/Alkan2011; 46br Dreamstime/Patrick Poendi; 47 NASA; 48l SPL/International Astronomical Union/Martin Kornmesser; 48cl SPL/US Geological Survey; 48c SPL/NASA; 49tr SPL/Claus Lunau/FOCI/Bonnier Publications; 49bl SPL/Detlev van Ravenswaay; 49c SPL/Mark Garlick; 49br SPL/Friedrich Saurer; 50–51 SPL/Mehau Kulkyk; 51tl Tim Van Sant, ST9 Solar Sail Team Lead, NASA Goddard Space Flight Center; 51c SPL/Scharmer et al, Royal Swedish Academy of Sciences; 51cb Corbis/Roger Ressmeyer; 51r SPL; 52t ESA/NASA; 52c SPL/US Geological Survey; 53tr SPL/NASA; 54tr SPL/Bernard Edmaier; 54c SPL/Colin Cuthbert; 55tl Corbis/Keren Su; 55c PA/AP; 55c and 55cr Corbis/Randy Wells; 55bl Alamy/Steve Bloom Images; 57tr SPL/NASA; 58tl Corbis/NASA/epa; 58cl Corbis/Reuters/NASA; 58cr SPL/NASA; 59tr Corbis/ Guido Cozzi; 60cl SPL/Mark Garlick; 61b SPL/Detlev van Ravenswaay; 62cl & tr NASA; 62bl Dreamstime/Xneo; 62br Dreamstime/Alexokokok; 63 iStock/m-gucci; 64tr Corbis/Bryan Allen; 64bl Getty/Taxi; 65b Kamioka Observatory, ICRR (Institute for Cosmic Ray Research), The University of Tokyo, Japan; 68br Science Photo Library (SPL)/Jerry Lodriguss; 69bl SPL/David A. Hardy, Futures: 50 Yrs in Space; 69br SPL/Allan Morton/Dennis Milon; 70bl SPL/J-C Cuillandre/Canada-France-Hawaii Telescope; 72tr SPL/Mark Garlick; 73tr SPL/Mark Garlick; 74cr SPL/NASA/ESA/R. Sahai & J. Trauger, JPL; 75tr; SPL/Russell Kightley; 75b SPL/Konstantinos Kifondis; 76tl & 80tl Dreamstime/Kojihirano; 76cl Dreamstime/Welcomia; 76bl NASA; 76tr Dreamstime/Lloyd Smith; 76br ESO.

CONTENTS

OUR
EARTH

EARTH IN SPACE

▼ PLANET – a large, round ball of rock, metal or gas in space that orbits a star, such as the Sun

Earth is a ball of rock spinning in space. It is one of eight planets that orbit (continually travels around) our Sun. The planets probably formed about 4.6 billion years ago from material left over after the Sun was born. Earth is very different from the other planets because it is the only one known to have life and liquid water on its surface. Forces inside planet Earth interact with the air, water, land and life on the surface to shape and change a unique world that is our home.

As the third planet from the Sun, Earth is neither too hot nor too cold but just the right temperature for life to survive. Far out in space, the huge planet Jupiter can act as a shield against space rocks that could destroy life on Earth.

Planet water

Nearly 70 per cent of Earth's surface is covered by water. The four biggest areas of water are the Arctic, Atlantic, Indian and Pacific Oceans. There are seven big areas of land (continents): Africa, Antarctica, Asia, Australia, Europe and North and South America. A blanket of gases called the atmosphere surrounds and protects Earth from the Sun's harmful rays and also from meteors. Swirling, white clouds of water form in the atmosphere as the Sun heats Earth's air and water, creating the weather.

> The Moon is about 384,400km from Earth; the Sun is about 150 million km away.

"...a sparkling blue and white jewel, a light, delicate sky-blue sphere laced with slowly swirling veils of white... a small pearl in a thick sea of black mystery. It takes more than a moment to fully realize this is Earth... home."

Edgar Mitchell (born 1930)
*American astronaut,
the sixth person to walk on the Moon*

http://science.nationalgeographic.com/science/space/solar-system/earth.html

The Moon

Earth has one moon, which is a ball of rock that orbits a planet. As well as orbiting Earth and travelling with the planet on its long journey around the Sun, the Moon spins on its own axis. The Moon pulls at Earth with a force called gravity. This stops our planet from wobbling too much, keeping the climate stable and allowing life to develop.

⊖ CHANGING SEASONS

As Earth travels around the Sun once a year, it tilts at an angle of 23.5°. This tilt makes the weather in some parts of the world change in a regular pattern called the seasons. In spring and summer seasons, these parts are tilted towards the Sun and are warmer. In autumn and winter, they are tilted away and are colder.

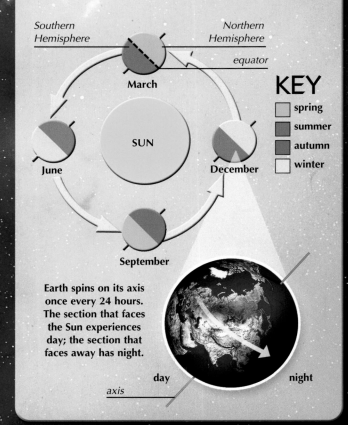

Southern Hemisphere

Northern Hemisphere

equator

March

SUN

June

December

September

KEY

spring
summer
autumn
winter

Earth spins on its axis once every 24 hours. The section that faces the Sun experiences day; the section that faces away has night.

day

night

axis

INSIDE EARTH

The surface layer of Earth, the crust, is like the thin skin of an apple. It is divided into about 14 large plates and 38 smaller ones, which fit together like the pieces of a jigsaw.

The cool, blue and white face on the outside of Earth hides a boiling hot inside, which may be nearly as hot as the surface of the Sun. Even Earth's surface is not quite what it seems. Unlike other planets, its thin surface layer is cracked into gigantic pieces called plates. The heat inside Earth makes these plates slip and slide about, pushing up mountains and volcanoes and causing earthquakes.

"Was I to believe him… in his intention to penetrate to the centre of this massive globe? Had I been listening to the mad speculations of a lunatic, or to the scientific conclusions of a lofty genius?"

Jules Verne (1828–1905)
French author writing in Journey to the Centre of the Earth *(1864)*

Growing and shrinking

Over time, Earth's rocky plates, which are 80–400km thick, change in size. They grow if material from inside Earth is added to their edges. They become smaller if they are crushed together or their edges sink back down inside Earth. This means the overall size of the crust stays the same.

● PLATES ON THE MOVE

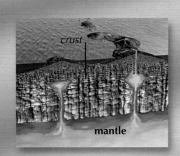

crust

mantle

Hot rocks from inside Earth may burn their way right through the middle of a plate to form islands in the ocean. The Hawaiian Islands were formed in this way.

Deep under the oceans, plates move apart. Hot rocks well up through the gaps and form long ridges of undersea mountains, such as those in the middle of the Atlantic and Pacific Oceans.

continental crust

oceanic crust

When two plates collide, one plate may be forced beneath the other, causing volcanoes above. The other plate may be pushed upwards to form mountains like the Himalayas.

As two plates slide and grind slowly past each other, the rocks may crack apart to form lines called fault lines. Earthquakes often happen along fault lines.

> Earth's plates slide across the globe at about the same speed as your fingernails grow: 1–10cm per year.

Drilling into Earth

Earth is made up of four main layers.
Deep in its centre, some 6,400km from
the surface, is the inner core, a solid ball
probably made of iron. Although the core
is unbelievably hot (3,000–5,000°C),
the pressure is so high that it cannot melt.
Around this is the slightly cooler outer
core, probably made of liquid iron, which
creates a magnetic field around Earth.
Next comes the mantle, the thickest layer,
making up 70–80 per cent of the planet.
The crust is the final and thinnest layer.
It ranges in thickness from 5–10km (oceanic
crust) to 15–70km (continental crust).

www.cotf.edu/ete/modules/msese/earthsysflr/plates1.html

*hot rock rises
towards crust,
where it cools*

*rock sinks
towards core,
where it heats
up again*

Inside the mantle,
the liquid rock is so hot
that it flows in circular
currents, which push
around the plates on
Earth's surface.

INNER CORE

OUTER CORE

MANTLE

CRUST

Tsunami

Earthquakes in the sea can set off enormous sea waves called tsunamis (*sue-naam-ees*). These huge waves travel across the oceans at up to 960km/h and can cross the Pacific Ocean in less than 24 hours. Near the coast, tsunamis can reach heights of 30m. In December 2004, an earthquake in the Indian Ocean triggered a tsunami that devastated many parts of the world.

A large amount of water is thrust upwards.

FOCUS

OCEANIC CRUST

The thinner, denser plate subducts, or moves beneath, the less dense plate.

A survivor of the 2004 tsunami stands amongst the rubble where his home once stood in Banda Aceh, Indonesia. The tsunami killed almost 300,000 people.

EARTHQUAKES

Earthquakes happen when a sudden release of energy in Earth's crust causes the ground to shake, sometimes violently. The Richter Scale can measure the amount of energy released by an earthquake, with catastrophic quakes recording over eight on the scale. The biggest earthquakes are caused by plate movements, but earthquakes can also be triggered by volcanic eruptions or artificial explosions. Every year, there are probably more than one million earthquakes, although many of these are very small and are not felt by people.

A crack in the crust called a fault forms as blocks of Earth's crust slide past each other during a quake. The focus is the underground starting point of the earthquake. Most damage occurs at the epicentre – the point on the surface directly above the focus.

> A severe earthquake can be 10,000 times more powerful than the first atomic bomb.

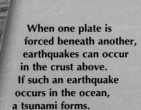

CONTINENTAL CRUST

When one plate is forced beneath another, earthquakes can occur in the crust above. If such an earthquake occurs in the ocean, a tsunami forms.

he thicker, less dense plate crumples upwards as it llides with the other plate.

fault line

Shock waves called seismic waves ripple out from the focus.

Moving and shaking

During an earthquake, Earth's rocks crack or shudder, causing shock waves, or seismic waves, that spread from the place where the quake started underground. This place is called the focus of the earthquake. The waves travel inside Earth and along its surface. Their speed depends on the depth of the focus and the strength of the rocks through which they move. Waves from very large earthquakes can cause the whole planet to ring like a tuning fork for an entire day.

Earthquakes often occur along fault lines, such as the San Andreas Fault (right) in California, USA. Faults are lines of weakness in Earth's crust.

www.guardian.co.uk/world/interactive/2008/jan/23/earthquakes

EPICENTRE

FOCUS

The focus of deep earthquakes may occur more than 700km below Earth's surface.

VOLCANOES

Volcanoes are openings on Earth's surface through which hot molten rock (magma), ash and gas escape. They release pressure building up under the ground and help to cool Earth's fiery core. Most of Earth's volcanoes occur along plate edges, where the crust is weakest and the magma can easily burst through. There are more than 500 active volcanoes in the world and one in ten people live in areas threatened by volcanic eruptions.

MAGMA – very hot, liquid (molten) rock from Earth's crust and mantle deep underground

In 1997, Plymouth, on the Caribbean island of Montserrat, was buried under more than 12m of mud and ash after a nearby volcano erupted. The town was abandoned permanently.

Fire mountain

When magma pours out of a volcano onto Earth's surface, it is called lava. This volcano has formed a mountain made of layers of ash and lava, which have cooled down and turned into hard rock. The shape of a volcano depends on the type of lava. Thick and sticky lava does not flow far before it goes solid, so it forms dome-shaped volcanoes. Thin and runny lava spreads out across wider areas to form low, flat shapes, called shield volcanoes.

1

> Red-hot lava, which can reach more than 1,000°C, flows out of a volcano at speeds of up to 180m/s.

In May 2008, Chile's Chaiten volcano erupted after 9,000 years, throwing clouds of ash more than 16km into the sky and depositing ash hundreds of kilometres away in Argentina.

KEY

1. **laccolith** – a chamber of magma that forces the rock above it into a dome shape

2. **magma chamber** – an underground pool of molten (liquid, melted) rock

3. **main vent** – the chimney through which magma escapes to the surface

4. **geyser** – a fountain of boiling hot water and steam, heated by hot volcanic rock

5. **hot spring** – water, also heated under the surface, that bubbles to the surface and colours the ground with its minerals

6. **fissure vent** – a long, thin crack, sometimes several kilometres in length, through which lava erupts

www.ready.gov/volcanoes

Robots collect samples of gases and rocks from volcanic areas that are too dangerous for people to reach.

2

3

4

5

6

MOUNTAINS

About one fifth of Earth's surface is made up of mountains. These steep-sided areas, usually over 1,000m tall, dominate the landscape around them. The world's biggest mountain ranges include the Alps of Europe, the Himalayas of Asia, the Rocky Mountains of North America and the Andes of South America. There are even huge mountains under the sea.

RANGE – a group or chain of mountains

Fold mountains

These mountains form when two of Earth's plates crash into each other, pushing up the layers of rocks between them into gigantic bends, called folds. The Himalayas are still being pushed upwards by about 6cm every year.

Fault-block mountains

Block mountains form when pressure beneath Earth's crust pushes huge chunks of land upwards between two cracks, or faults, in the crust. Like most block mountains, Table Mountain in South Africa has a flat top, not the jagged peaks of fold mountains.

BLOCK MOVES UP

BLOCK MOVES DOWN

fault line

Volcanic mountain Mauna Kea, Hawaii, is 10,205m high (taller than Everest), but about 6,000m of it lies under the ocean.

Bar-headed geese fly over the Himalayas from feeding grounds in India to nesting sites in Tibet. They can extract oxygen from the very thin mountain air.

Dome mountains

Sometimes magma pushes up the crust without folding or faulting it, or breaking through to the surface. When this occurs, the land bulges upwards into a rounded shape called a dome mountain.

LACCOLITH

MAGMA CHAMBER

PLATES MOVING TOGETHER

Volcanic mountains

Volcanic mountains, such as Mount Kilimanjaro in East Africa, form when magma from beneath the crust escapes onto the surface and builds up, layer upon layer, into a huge mound of rock.

Making mountains

Mountains are pushed upwards by the movements of Earth's plates or by magma from deep inside the mantle forcing its way through the crust. Mountains are evidence of forces inside our planet that are strong enough to move enormous areas of rocks over millions of years. Some mountains are still growing taller, while others are being worn away and will one day be flat land again.

Mount Kilimanjaro, an extinct volcano, is 5,895m tall and is the highest mountain in Africa. It lies in Tanzania, about 322km south of the equator.

"Mountains are the beginning and the end of all natural scenery."

John Ruskin (1819–1900)
British art critic and author

MINERAL – a natural substance in Earth's crust that has a constant chemical composition and a particular crystal structure

Standing stones

In Nambung National Park, Western Australia, stand thousands of spectacular limestone pillars, some of them 4m tall. The pillars are all that remains of a thick layer of hard limestone rock that formed under sand dunes. Over thousands of years, the wind blew away the loose sand to reveal the columns of rock.

ROCKS AND MINERALS

Rocks are the solid materials of Earth's crust. They are full of clues about our planet's past because their characteristics depend on how and where they were formed. All rocks are made of mixtures of natural chemicals, called minerals, which usually form crystals and are stuck together in a solid chunk. There are three main types of rocks: igneous, sedimentary and metamorphic.

Igneous rocks

These rocks are formed when magma escapes through cracks in the crust and cools and hardens on the surface. The Giant's Causeway in Ireland (above) was created about 60 million years ago by volcanoes that erupted, leaving a lava pond. The 40,000 columns formed as the lava cooled, shrank and cracked. Most of the columns are six-sided.

> Coal is made from dead swamp plants pressed tightly together over millions of years.

Sedimentary rocks

These rocks are made from sediments – small grains of sand, mud and other debris removed from rocks by wind or water. They are also made from the remains of plants or animals. The sediments collect in layers on the bottom of seas, lakes and rivers. Eventually, the weight of all the layers squeezes out the water, pressing the sediments into solid rock such as sandstone, limestone or chalk.

www.geolsoc.org.uk/rockcycle

⊜ THE ROCK CYCLE

Rocks are continually forming, being destroyed and remade in a recycling process called the rock cycle. New rocks form when volcanoes erupt, but old rocks are eroded, or worn away, by wind or water. Old rocks can be changed into new ones by pressure, heat and forces inside Earth.

IGNEOUS ROCK

weathering, erosion

heat, pressure

cooling, solidifying

melting

compacting

weathering, erosion

sediments

melting

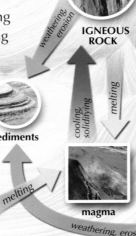

magma

weathering, erosion

melting

SEDIMENTARY ROCK

heat, pressure

METAMORPHIC ROCK

Metamorphic rocks

When igneous or sedimentary rocks are baked by red-hot magma or squeezed by powerful plate movements, metamorphic rock is created. The sedimentary rock limestone changes with heat and pressure into the metamorphic rock marble (below).

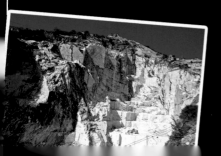

Minerals

Minerals are basic natural substances usually made of two or more chemical elements, such as oxygen, silicon, calcium, iron or sodium. Minerals form when the elements in a gas or a liquid change into solid shapes with flat sides and angled edges, called crystals.

Quartz, a very common mineral, is a major ingredient of most igneous and metamorphic rocks.

Hematite is made of iron and oxygen and has been mined as a source of iron since ancient times.

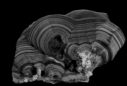

Malachite often has distinctive green bands. The bright green tarnish on copper is malachite.

INVESTIGATE

Discover more about our planet and how it evolved by checking out visitor attractions, geological sites, museums, books and websites.

Stromboli, an island volcano in Italy, has been erupting for the last 2,000 years.

Sites and visitor centres

From a local beach to an active volcano, there are sites all over the world that you can visit to see geology in action first hand.

 Volcanoes and Earthquakes by Kathy Furgang (National Geographic Kids)

 Parco dell'Etna, Sicily, Italy

 www.bbc.co.uk/education/clips/zrd9wmn

crystals of the mineral aragonite

Books and magazines

Visitor centres, museums and libraries are great places to check out the huge range of reading material you can use to learn more about our planet.

 Frozen Planet by Alastair Fothergill and Vanessa Berlowitz (BBC Books)

 Our Dynamic Earth, 112–116 Holyrood Gait, Edinburgh, Midlothian EH8 8AS

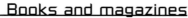 www.kidsastronomy.com/earth.htm

The Matterhorn straddles the border between Italy and Switzerland.

Museums and exhibitions

Museums, local, national and online, regularly stage science exhibitions and have interactive displays to help you understand how our planet works.

 Understanding Earth by John Grotzinger and Thomas H. Jordan (W. H. Freeman)

 British Geological Survey, Natural History Museum, Cromwell Road, London SW7 5BD

 www.sciencekids.co.nz/sciencefacts/earth.html

Basalt columns form the Giant's Causeway in Northern Ireland.

Documentaries and movies

Dramatic documentaries on television or movies at the cinema, on DVD and online can take you into the heart of an earthquake or right to the rim of a volcano.

 Planet Earth (BBC DVD)

 Grand Canyon National Park, Grand Canyon Village, AZ 86023, United States

www.windows2universe.org/earth/earth.html

A WORLD
OF WATER

WATERY PLANET

Most of us probably think of our world as being solid ground, but 71 per cent of the planet's surface is actually covered by salt water. The largest areas of this water, between the continents, are called oceans. Areas of salt water closer to the land, or partly or completely surrounded by land, are called seas.

World ocean

There are five oceans: the Pacific Ocean, Atlantic Ocean, Indian Ocean, Southern Ocean and Arctic Ocean. Channels of water link these oceans to form one gigantic body of water. The Pacific is larger than the other four oceans put together, reaching halfway around the world.

⊖ WATER CYCLE

The oceans exchange water with the atmosphere in a never-ending cycle. Heat from the sun turns water at the sea's surface into water vapour. This rises into the sky where it cools and turns back to droplets of water that form clouds. The clouds spill rain and snow, which form streams, rivers and glaciers that flow back to the ocean. Even the water that seeps into the ground finds its way back to the sea.

water freezes and falls as snow

wind blows cloud inland

plants lose water to the air

water vapour rises from the ocean

rain falls on the ocean

water vapour rises from lakes

rivers and streams flow into the ocean

Rains wash salt out of the rocks and into rivers, which carry it to the sea. This makes the sea salty.

Ocean trade link

Every year, about 50,000 ships carrying one-quarter of the world's freight use the Strait of Malacca as a short-cut between the Pacific and Indian Oceans. The channel is one of the busiest shipping routes in the world.

Sea feature

About 300,000km^2 of seabed below the warm, shallow waters of the tropics are covered in hedge-like structures called coral reefs. The Great Barrier Reef in the Pacific Ocean, off the coast of Australia, is the world's largest coral reef system.

 > The Southern Ocean was declared an ocean by the International Hydrographic Organization in 2000

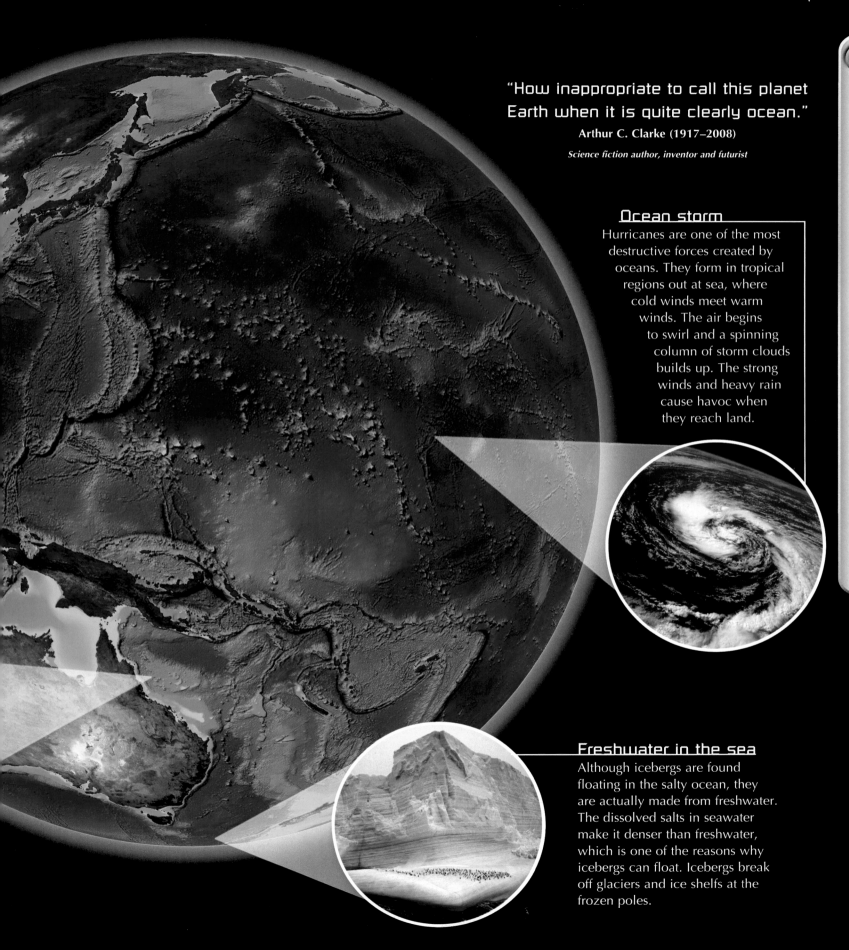

"How inappropriate to call this planet
Earth when it is quite clearly ocean."

Arthur C. Clarke (1917–2008)

Science fiction author, inventor and futurist

http://school.discoveryeducation.com/schooladventures/planetocean/ocean.html

Ocean storm

Hurricanes are one of the most destructive forces created by oceans. They form in tropical regions out at sea, where cold winds meet warm winds. The air begins to swirl and a spinning column of storm clouds builds up. The strong winds and heavy rain cause havoc when they reach land.

Freshwater in the sea

Although icebergs are found floating in the salty ocean, they are actually made from freshwater. The dissolved salts in seawater make it denser than freshwater, which is one of the reasons why icebergs can float. Icebergs break off glaciers and ice shelfs at the frozen poles.

ANCIENT OCEANS

FOSSIL – mineralized remains or the impression of ancient animals and plants

The first ocean on Earth was formed very early in the planet's 4.6-billion-year history. The oldest known rocks, which have features that show they originally formed on an ocean floor, are dated to about 4 billion years ago. This means one global ocean probably existed before the continents. It was split up by continents forming from volcanic eruptions and slowly drifting across the face of the planet on moving plates of Earth's crust.

Gases and water vapour from inside Earth erupt from the volcano.

Single-celled algae were floating in the sunlit areas of the oceans from about 2 billion years ago.

Earliest ocean

Most of the water on Earth was probably released as water vapour by volcanoes and vents roughly 4.2 billion years ago. Eventually the vapour cooled into rain that poured down to create a global ocean. Fossils of sea-living cyanobacteria show that there was life in the ocean at least 3.5 billion years ago. We know cyanobacteria formed stony structures, called stromatolites, because the bacteria still form these structures today.

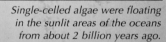

> The Atlantic Ocean is getting wider by 25mm per year.

High and dry

The really interesting thing about this fossil of a sea-dwelling ammonite is that it was found in rocks high up in the Himalayas in Asia. This proves that the mountains were once part of the sea floor. They formed when India drifted north and crashed into Asia, pushing seabed rocks 8km into the air.

A meteorite brings water in the form of vapour to the planet.

Rivers of lava contain water vapour from deep inside Earth.

Vents in the seabed spit out boiling hot water.

Mats of cyanobacteria build in layers to form a stromatolite.

⊜ DRIFTING APART

240 million years ago

One giant ocean, Panthalassa, surrounded the supercontinent Pangaea 290–240 million years ago (mya). Then Pangaea broke up, with one part drifting north and one part south. The northern part split to form the North Atlantic 208–146 mya. From 146 mya, the South Atlantic and Indian Oceans began to form. The oceans are still changing shape today.

208 million years ago

146 million years ago

today

UNDER THE SEA

Just a century ago, very little was known about the ocean floor. Following the invention of sonar and echo-sounding equipment in the 1920s and deep-sea diving craft in the 1930s, we now know the ocean floor is a world of great plains, huge mountains, active volcanoes and deep chasms, called trenches. Many of these are formed by the movement of the tectonic plates that make up Earth's crust.

SUBDUCTION ZONE – an area where one tectonic plate is diving beneath another into the interior of the Earth

An island is formed when the summit of a volcano rises above the surface of the water.

A volcanic island arc forms where tectonic plates meet.

Deep trenches occur where two plates push against each other and one slides under the other.

A seamount is an extinct volcano that does not rise above the surface of the water.

Ocean floor

Much of the ocean floor is a flat plain, covered with a deep layer of fine particles, called ooze. Chains of underwater mountains run the length of all oceans. Along each ridge, lava bubbles up and cools to form new sea floor as plates move away on either side. Trenches descend in subduction zones where plates collide. Here, volcanoes have burst up to create seamounts. Some of these reach the ocean surface as volcanic islands.

Hot, soft mantle moves slowly like a conveyor belt, carrying plates of crust.

> Standing at 10,205m, Mouna Kea in the Pacific Ocean is the highest underwater mountain.

Continental slope

At the edges of the continents the sea is quite shallow and is a hunting ground for seabirds, but usually within a few kilometres of land the seabed starts to slope downwards into the black depths.

A mid-ocean ridge is formed where plates pull apart and magma rises up to fill the gaps, creating new ocean floor.

Hydrothermal vents

Dark plumes of hot, mineral-rich water gush out of hydrothermal vents in Earth's crust. Over time the minerals settle around the vents to form chimneys.

Deep dive

In 1960, the US Navy sent the *Trieste* submersible down into the Mariana Trench in the Pacific Ocean. It took almost five hours to complete the descent to the bottom, which was almost 11km down.

⊖ SONAR

Scientists on board ships use sonar to map the ocean floor. The scientists direct sound waves at the bottom, and chart the echoes that bounce back to create images, such as this one, of an area of the Pacific's mid-ocean ridge. Different colours show different depths. Dark blue is the deepest; red is the shallowest.

map created from sonar data

RIVERS AND COASTS

The water in rivers and oceans is a powerful force that shapes the surface of planet Earth. It can break up rocks and soil, carrying them away to carve valleys, caves, bays and headlands. And it can deposit the rocks and soil as sediment to form floodplains, deltas, beaches and saltmarshes. The gradual breaking down of rocks by the weather, plants or chemicals is called weathering. The carrying away of this rocky material by wind, water or moving rivers of ice (glaciers) is called erosion.

DELTA – a build-up of sediments deposited by a river when its current slows as it meets the sea

● SHAPING THE COAST

As waves crash against the shore, throwing sand and pebbles at soft rock, bays are carved into the coastline. Harder rock survives to stick out as headlands. If waves hollow out caves on either side of a headland, a rock arch forms. And if the top of the arch collapses, a tall pillar called a stack is left.

saltmarsh – plants grow in shallow, protected water

dunes

headland

bay

arch

cave

stack

spit – ridge formed by longshore drift moving material out to sea

lagoon – coastal lake cut off from sea by sand bar

estuary – wide mouth of river on coast

arrows show longshore drift – sideways movement of beach material if waves strike coast at an angle

Mangroves

In the Everglades National Park, Florida, USA, mangroves help to protect the coast from strong waves and storms. Their tangled, stilt-like roots trap mud, helping to build up new land. The roots also anchor the muddy soil during hurricanes.

River Nile's delta

In 1971, a dam was built across the River Nile near the city of Aswan. The dam generates electricity and irrigates crops, but it also stops the river carrying sediments down to the delta. Now the outer edges of the delta are being worn away by the sea and the soil is becoming more salty.

> Tides are caused by the pull of gravity from the Moon and the Sun, whereas waves are driven by the wind.

Water highways

As a river winds to and fro across the land, like a natural highway carrying water and sediments instead of cars, it can carve sharp bends called meanders. The precise shape and path of the river and its side channels depend on the type of soil and rock around it as well as on the slope of the land.

This river, in Kimberley, Western Australia, meanders across a floodplain.

is false-colour satellite age shows the fan-shaped ta of the River Nile in Egypt.

www.bbc.co.uk/schools/riversandcoasts

ICE SHEET – *a vast layer of ice that forms only over land*

"Deeply regret [to] advise you: Titanic sank this morning after collision with iceberg, resulting in serious loss of life. Full particulars later."

Joseph Bruce Ismay (1862–1937)
Survivor of the sinking of the RMS Titanic sending a message to New York after the 1912 disaster

Rivers of ice

A glacier forms when snow piles up in a mountain valley and, at its base, becomes squeezed into ice – like pressing soft snow to make an icy snowball. The glacier is pulled downhill by gravity, causing deep cracks on its surface. Eventually, the glacier reaches warmer places and slowly melts, depositing the rocks and soil it has been carrying.

Sawyer Glacier, Alaska, USA

ICE SHEETS AND GLACIERS

Earth's water is strange stuff. As well as existing in liquid form, it also turns into a solid called ice when temperatures drop below freezing. The largest continuous area of ice in the world is the vast ice sheet covering the continent of Antarctica. The North Pole is surrounded by a huge frozen ocean, the Arctic Ocean, and down from the tops of Earth's cold mountains, rivers of ice called glaciers slowly flow. As the glaciers move along, they dig up rocks and carry them down the mountains, carving valleys into deep 'U' shapes.

A group of visitors to Antarctica view a huge, overturned iceberg near to Enterprise Island.

> Ice covers about 10 per cent of Earth's land and about 12 per cent of its oceans.

Clues in the rock

As a glacier moves along, pieces of rock trapped in the ice grind and scrape away at the ground like sandpaper, leaving scars on the landscape. These scars indicate the size and flow direction of glaciers that passed over the rock long ago. Thicker glaciers press down harder and carve out deeper grooves than thinner glaciers.

STUDYING GLACIERS

A scientist who studies glaciers, and ice in general, is called a glaciologist. Like frozen chunks of history, glaciers can tell scientists about Earth's climate in the past. Their size, shape and speed can also tell scientists about today's climate. About 75 per cent of Earth's fresh water is locked away in glaciers and ice sheets.

This glaciologist is using crampons and ice axes to haul himself up a glacier to examine its structure.

Icebergs

In the cold polar regions at the top and bottom of the world, huge chunks of ice break off glaciers and ice sheets and float away into the oceans as icebergs. Ice only just floats on water, so about 90 per cent of an iceberg is hidden under the water. The hidden part of the iceberg is very dangerous to ships in polar waters.

WEATHER AND WATER

The Sun's heat stirs up Earth's atmosphere, making air and water move from place to place. This creates clouds, winds and all sorts of weather. The weather on planet Earth changes all the time, mainly because of all the water on the surface. The world's water is never used up. It just moves from the land or the oceans up into the sky and back down again in a never-ending loop called the water cycle.

Cumulus clouds look like fluffy cotton wool.

satellite photograph of the northern hemisphere's jet stream carrying clouds over Egypt and the Red Sea

Icy cirrus clouds mark the position of a strong wind called a jet stream, which blows at over 200km/h about 10km above Earth. There are two jet streams – one in each hemisphere – and they move large masses of air. This has a major impact on the world's weather.

Condensation

As the air full of water vapour rises it cools down because temperatures decrease higher up. Cool air cannot hold as much water vapour as warm air, so some of the vapour turns back into droplets of water. This process of a gas changing into a liquid when it cools is called condensation. The droplets of condensed water gather to form clouds.

Evaporation

When liquid water is heated, it turns into an invisible gas called water vapour and disappears into the air. This process of a liquid changing into a gas when it is heated is called evaporation. The warm air containing the evaporated water is less dense, and therefore lighter, than the liquid water, so it rises up into the sky.

When water vapour in the air condenses onto cold glass, drops of water form. A similar process occurs inside clouds.

> Each raindrop is made up of a million cloud droplets.

Precipitation

Clouds are made up of masses of tiny water droplets hanging in the sky. When the droplets bump into each other, they form large drops of water that are too heavy to stay in the cloud. This causes precipitation – water falling as rain, snow or hail.

In very cold air, water droplets freeze into tiny ice crystals, which stick together to make snowflakes.

Water vapour and clouds are blown by the wind, so rain often falls a long distance from where the water first evaporated.

http://kids.earth.nasa.gov/droplet.html

Transpiration is the process by which water evaporates from plants, mainly through their leaves.

Infiltration is the process of water seeping down through rocks and soil.

The 'groundwater' reaches a layer that won't absorb it and moves downhill to the sea.

The surface of the groundwater is the water table.

The water cycle

When the Sun heats the water in the oceans, on the land or in living things, the water evaporates into the air and rises up into the sky. There, it cools down and condenses to form clouds, which release the water as rain or snow. When the Sun heats the water on the surface, the cycle starts all over again.

INVESTIGATE

You can find out more about the oceans by visiting aquariums and museums as well as checking out books and websites.

an iceberg floating in Franz Joseph Fjord in Greenland

Aquarium research

Enjoy the entertainment and exhibits at an aquarium, but take time to learn about the oceans from the research undertaken there.

a view of the Earth with the Red Sea near the centre of the image

 Oceans by Anne Laking and Paul Rose (BBC Books)

 The Oceanografic, Autopista del Saler 5, Valencia 46103, Spain

https://scripps.ucsd.edu/explorations/voyager

Books and magazines

You can find lots of information about our watery world in books and magazines in a public library or museum library.

 Weird Sea Creatures by Laura Marsh (National Geographic Society)

 The Natural History Museum, Cromwell Road, London SW7 5BD

a mangrove tree growing in shallow, tropical ba...

http://environment.nationalgeographic.com/environment/habitats/

Museums and exhibitions

To discover more about water, the oceans and creatures that live in the sea, try paying a visit to a museum or an exhibition at an aquarium.

 Coral Reefs: Secret Cities of the Sea by Anne Sheppard (Natural History Museum)

 Sea Life London Aquarium, County Hall, Westminster Bridge Road, London SE1 7PB

A river winds through the Kaimanawa Ranges in New Zealand.

http://ocean.si.edu

Documentaries and movies

The greatest oceanographic experts have sailed around the world to create films that you can watch from the comfort of your living room.

 The Blue Planet (BBC DVD)

 Search on 'oceanography' to find film clips and documentaries on the Internet.

  www.kidsgeo.com/index.php

HABITATS

DESERTS

The driest places on the planet (usually with less than 25 centimetres of rain a year), deserts cover almost one third of the land surface. During the day, they are baking hot, but at night, temperatures can plummet to below freezing because there are few clouds or plants to hold heat near the ground. High winds, bare rocks, shifting sand dunes and rare floods make deserts hostile environments for living things.

This giant saguaro cactus, in the Sonoran Desert, Arizona, USA, grew its arms when it was 75 years old – it may live for over 200 years. When it rains, the pleats in its stem expand like a concertina, allowing the cactus to take in as much water as possible.

Oases

In a few places in a desert, water comes to the surface to form a moist area called an oasis. The water often comes from rain that falls on mountains far away and travels underground through rocks that hold water. A pool of water collects in a hollow that dips below the top of the water table.

Crescent Lake is a natural oasis in the Gobi Desert in China. However, artificial oases can be created by digging wells in places where the water table is close to the surface.

Plantlife

Plants have to be very tough to survive in deserts because they can't hide from the sun as animals do. They store water in their stems and leaves, and soak up moisture with wide-spreading roots that tap into water deep underground. Some plants survive when their seeds are buried in the desert soil. The seeds lie in wait for a rare rainstorm to help them sprout.

> There is enough water in a giant saguaro cactus to fill 1,000 bathtubs!

Desert dunes

In some deserts, such as the Sahara, the wind blows sand into vast areas called sand seas or ergs. Within the ergs, heaps of sand, or dunes, move with the wind, changing shape like waves on the sea. The shape of a dune depends on the amount of sand as well as the wind speed and direction. Crescent-shaped barchan dunes form where the wind blows from the same direction. Seif dunes are steep ridges of sand.

"One day, we had to advance in the teeth of the [sand]storm... To stop means to be drowned by the sand. The camels instinctively know this and continue to advance in spite of the tormenting blast."

Ahmed Hassanein (1889–1946)
Egyptian politican and explorer writing about his travels in the Libyan Desert

Sand dunes in the Sahara Desert, the biggest desert in the world, cover an area almost as big as the USA.

● DESERT ANIMALS

Most desert animals survive with very little water, often getting all the water they need from their food. Kangaroo rats don't drink at all. They hide from the heat of the day in burrows, emerging in the cool of the night to search for food. Camels store fat in their humps and break this down to provide food and water when needed. A camel has wide feet to stop it sinking into the sand and long eyelashes to keep sand out of its eyes.

The scaly skin of reptiles, such as this chameleon, prevents water loss. Reptiles can survive higher temperatures than birds or mammals.

The big ears of the sand fox work like radiators to transfer heat into the air to cool the animal.

Tropical grasslands

One of the two main types of grassland is the tropical savannah of Africa, India and Australia. Some of the largest animals on the planet – elephants and giraffes – live on the African savannah. These warm grasslands have wet and dry seasons, and animals move around following the rains, which help fresh grass to grow.

Land of the llama

Grasslands grow on flat plains high in the Andes mountains of South America. They are grazed by llamas, which were tamed by the Incas some 6,000 years ago. They are still used for carrying supplies today, as well as for their wool and meat.

GRASSLANDS

Covering about a quarter of the planet, grasslands grow in between regions of wet forests and dry deserts. Few trees survive in grasslands, because either the weather is too dry or the soils are too poor. In some areas, grazing animals or fires stop young trees from growing, allowing grasslands to spread. Grasslands are home to large grass-eating animals (grazers), such as antelope, as well as the predators that feed on them and the scavengers that clean up their leftovers. Small animals burrow beneath grasslands to hide from predators.

> Termite nests can contain up to 20 million individual termites and can be as tall as a giraffe.

● COOL GRASSLANDS

Cooler, temperate grasslands are found in Asia (the steppes), South America (the pampas) and North America (the prairies). Temperate grasslands usually develop in the middle of continents or in the rain shadow of high mountains where rainfall is low. People use temperate grasslands to graze animals or to grow crops such as wheat and corn.

This farmer is using camels to cut grass for making hay on the steppes of Mongolia, Asia.

Blazing grasslands

Fires are often started by lightning storms at the end of the dry season. Dry grasses catch fire easily and burn quickly. Fires destroy most trees and other large, slow-growing plants, but grasses soon sprout back. People sometimes start fires to encourage grasses to grow and create more land for crops or grazing cattle.

Zebras live in large herds on the African grasslands. These wild, striped horses bite off the tough tops of grasses, encouraging new shoots to grow from the base of the plants.

Termite mounds on the African savannah provide food for bat-eared foxes. The foxes use their keen hearing to find the termites, before licking them up.

ermite territory

nsects called termites construct huge nests n tropical grasslands. They build them with oil, saliva and droppings, which set to form rock-hard shelter from the heat. Millions of ermites live inside, eating decaying material r using it as compost to farm fungi for food.

bat-eared foxes

www.panda.org/about_our_earth/ecoregions/about/habitat_types/habitats/grasslands/

FORESTS

Thousands of years ago, forests covered about half of planet Earth's land, but today they cover less than a third. Forests are cut down for their wood and other natural resources, and to make space for farms and towns. Yet forests provide food, water and shelter for a huge variety of wildlife. They cool the planet by giving shade, recycle water through their leaves and regulate the amount of oxygen and carbon dioxide in the atmosphere. Without forests, the planet would be a much more hostile environment for life.

Rainforest roof

Most of the wildlife in a rainforest lives in the roof of the forest, called the canopy, which is about 40m above the ground. This layer receives the most rain and sun, which means it has the most leaves, flowers and fruits for animals such as monkeys and birds to eat.

A few very tall trees emerge from the canopy to form the 'emergent layer'.

Rainforests

These tropical forests grow in a band around the equator, where the weather is hot and wet all year round. They cover only 6 per cent of Earth's land surface, but more than half of the world's different species of living things live there. There are four main areas of rainforest: in Central and South America, in Africa, in Southeast Asia and in Australasia.

9

8

7

5

6

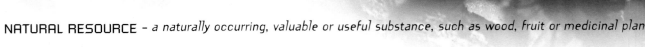

> NATURAL RESOURCE - a naturally occurring, valuable or useful substance, such as wood, fruit or medicinal plan

OTHER FORESTS

The two main types of cooler forests are the deciduous and coniferous forests in northern regions. They are dominated by the changing seasons. In the winter, animals migrate to warmer places further south or hide in burrows. A few animals hibernate, or sleep through the winter.

Coniferous trees have needle-shaped leaves to help snow slide off in winter. The trees produce seeds in cones.

Deciduous trees, unlike coniferous ones, have wide, flat leaves that change colour and fall off in autumn.

KEY

1. forest floor – a dark and gloomy layer (receiving only 1–2 per cent of sunlight), with a carpet of dead leaves

2. goliath tarantula – the largest spider in the world; feeds on frogs, lizards, mice and small snakes

3. jaguar – a large hunter that silently stalks wild pigs, rats, deer and armadillos along rainforest trails

4. understorey – a shady layer with insects, a tangle of vines and small trees and animals

5. leafcutter ants – they carry leaf pieces to nests under the ground to make compost to grow fungus for food

6. emerald tree boa – camouflaged among the green leaves, this snake snatches prey in its sharp teeth

7. drip tip – this long point on a leaf helps rainwater to drip away, stopping harmful algae from growing

8. epiphyte – a plant, such as this bromeliad, that perches on the branches of trees to get nearer to the light

9. red howler monkey – it calls out to warn other howlers to stay off its patch; it's hard to see through the thick forest, so sound is useful for communication

The tallest tree in the world, a giant sequoia, is more than 112m tall – the height of a 37-storey building!

MISTY AND MYSTERIOUS

Inside a rainforest, huge trees tower up into a mass of leaves high above. The leaves block out the sunlight, but not the heat. The air is hot and still, and very humid, because there is heavy rain every day. The misty warmth gives perfect conditions for plants to grow – and these are home to an amazing variety of animals. More species of wildlife live in the rainforest than in any other place on Earth. But this precious habitat is under threat, as vast areas are cleared to make way for farmland, roads and mines.

Canopy

A rainforest has several different layers. At the top is the tangled canopy of leaves and branches. There is more sunlight up here, and the trees grow leaves, fruits and seeds throughout the year. Most animals live in the canopy, because there is plenty of food and few large predators. In fact, many animals never go down to the forest floor at all.

Understorey

Stretching between the lower canopy and the ground is the very damp and hot understorey. Only about 5 per cent of sunlight reaches here, so many plants grow bigger leaves to catch whatever light there is. With fewer branches, there is space for insects and birds to fly around. Snakes and lizards move up and down the bare tree trunks.

> HUMID - *moist or damp (in the air)*

1 quetzal – a bird worshipped as a god by the ancient Aztec people, who lived in Mexico

2 Queen Alexandra's birdwing – the largest butterfly in the world, with wings up to 28cm across

3 jaguar – hunts for prey in rivers as well as on the forest floor

4 giant leaf-tailed gecko – has a flat tail shaped like a leaf and, when threatened, it stands up and hisses loudly

5 mandrill – one of the most colourful of all mammals, with bright blue and red swellings on the face and rump

6 rafflesia – produces the world's largest flowers, up to 90cm across, but it smells of rotting meat

Forest floor

There is very little light here, and few plants can grow. Leaves and other litter fall from the trees above and cover the ground, where they rot down quickly in the humid conditions. Huge numbers of insects live among the leaf litter, including ants and termites. A few large mammals, such as anteaters and jaguars, hunt for food on the forest floor.

People of the rainforest

Small groups of people live in rainforests. They have learned how to survive in this difficult environment. Their bodies are smaller and better at keeping cool. Most rainforest dwellers are nomads who move from place to place. They are skilful hunters, and they also gather wild fruits and vegetables.

❯ More than 70 per cent of the world's plant and animal species live in rainforests, and many of them are still undiscovered.

Penguins at the South Pole

Penguins and polar bears never meet because penguins live only in and around Antarctica, while polar bears live in northern Arctic lands. Penguins spend most of their lives at sea, using their stiff flippers to 'fly' underwater. Their dense, waterproof feathers and thick layers of fatty blubber keep the birds warm. Penguins come onto land or sea ice in order to breed, often forming huge colonies of up to a million birds.

A short, stubby tail is used as a prop to help penguins stand up and as a rudder for steering underwater.

colony of
Emperor penguins
in Antarctica

POLAR LANDS

The coldest places on the planet are at the top and bottom of the world – the Arctic is a frozen ocean around the North Pole, and Antarctica is a frozen continent around the South Pole. They both have bitterly cold winters and short, warm summers, when the Sun never sets. The poles are ringed by areas of tundra. Many animals visit polar lands in summer to feed and raise their young, but only a few very hardy animals, such as polar bears, can survive in polar lands all year round.

Summer holidays

Huge herds of reindeer, or caribou, are summer visitors to the flat, treeless tundra lands around the Arctic. They spend the winter feeding and sheltering in conifer forests further south. In the summer, they migrate, trekking thousands of kilometres to the tundra, where there is food and few predators.

> Most polar fish have a natural chemical 'anti-freeze' in their blood, which stops them from freezing solid in the icy water.

www.spri.cam.ac.uk/resources/kids

he chicks huddle together for
armth during snow blizzards.
heir parents make long journeys
o and from the sea to collect fish
or them. They recognize their
hicks by their high-pitched calls.

⊖ CAMOUFLAGE

The thick fur coat of the Arctic fox changes colour to hide the fox in its habitat as it hunts for prey such as birds or voles. This is camouflage. In winter, when the ground is snowy and icy, the fox grows thick white fur. In the summer, the white fur is replaced by a thinner coat of brownish-grey fur. This camouflages the fox against the brown and grey rocks and soil that appear as the snow and ice melt.

Arctic fox in summer

Arctic fox in winter

Polar plants
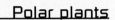

No plants grow at the snowy poles, but some tough plants live on the bleak tundra, where the snow and ice melts in summer. Simple plants, such as mosses and lichens, survive the intense cold, thin, frozen soils and short growing season. They grow in low 'cushions' to keep out of the wind and trap moisture.

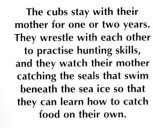

The cubs stay with their mother for one or two years. They wrestle with each other to practise hunting skills, and they watch their mother catching the seals that swim beneath the sea ice so that they can learn how to catch food on their own.

he ice bear

n the middle of the Arctic winter, a mother polar bear gives birth to two iny cubs inside a snow den. For six months, she stays hidden away, while her cubs drink her rich milk. She cannot leave the den to eat until the cubs are strong enough to go outside. She survives by using the energy stored in her thick body fat, which also keeps her warm.

OCEANS

The oceans cover more than 70 per cent of the planet and include the Pacific, Atlantic, Indian, Southern and Arctic Oceans as well as smaller seas. Under the oceans lies a dramatic landscape of huge mountain ranges, deep valleys and vast plains. Oceans have a huge impact on the weather, absorbing heat and spreading it around the world with its ocean currents.

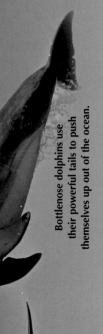

Bottlenose dolphins use their powerful tails to push themselves up out of the ocean.

The sunlit zone

This zone receives the most light and heat. It extends from the surface down to about 100–150m. This is the only zone in which plants can grow. Predators such as dolphins, sharks and tuna hunt in the sunlit zone.

Whale sharks, the biggest fish in the world, feed only on tiny drifting plants and animals called plankton.

The twilight zone

It is quite light in the upper part of the twilight zone during the day, but the lower part – some 1,000m beneath the surface – is always dark. The Sun's rays cannot reach this deep into the ocean and many animals produce their own light for camouflage, or to find food or mates. Animals feed on each other or on animal and plant remains that

The green sea turtle has powerful flippers to 'fly' underwater. It spends most of its life in the oceans, but females lay their eggs on beaches.

The building blocks of coral reefs are the skeletons of tiny anemone-like animals called polyps. Living polyps colonize the skeletons. The polyps can live only in clean, warm, salty water less than 30m deep as the algae living in them need sunlight to make food.

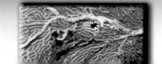

> OCEAN CURRENT – a 'river' of water flowing through the oceans, both near the surface and in the deep ocean

Zones of life

There is life at all levels in the oceans, from the sunlit surface to the deep darkness of the ocean floor. In each zone, creatures are specially adapted to the different conditions of temperature, light and salinity (saltiness of the water). Most sea creatures live in the top 100–150m, but some do move from one zone to another.

The giant isopod looks much like its woodlouse relative – but it is the size of a brick! It lives in the Antarctic Ocean and scavenges for scraps of food on the seabed.

With ear-like fins on top of its body, the dumbo octopus is named after Walt Disney's flying elephant. It lives at depths of 3,000–4,000m, hovering above the sea floor to hunt worms, shellfish and other prey.

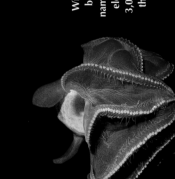

Anglerfish have a built-in 'fishing rod' with a glowing tip to lure prey towards them.

The weedy sea dragon, a type of seahorse, is well camouflaged by fleshy flaps that resemble seaweed.

The dark zone

The vast, completely dark zone of the deep ocean stretches down to 6,000m or more. Sea cucumbers dominate the ocean floor, sucking food scraps from the surface of the mud. Many deep-sea animals, such as sponges, sea anemones and tube worms, sit and wait for food to fall down on them from the zones above.

Superhot water gushes out of vents in black plumes. Bacteria get their energy from the chemicals in these 'black smokers' and provide food for animals such as giant tube worms. Vent bacteria can withstand higher temperatures than any other living thing.

On the ocean floor, a polystyrene cup shrinks to about the size of a thimble due to the crushing pressure.

INVESTIGATE

Find out more about different habitats by visiting safari parks, zoos and museums as well as checking out books and websites.

a Bengal Tiger in its forest habitat

Zoos and safari parks

A trip to a safari park or zoo allows you to see how animals have evolved to survive in different environments.

 Navigators: Killer Creatures by Claire Llewellyn (Kingfisher)

 Bristol Zoo Gardens, Clifton, Bristol BS8 3HA

 www.woburnsafari.co.uk

coral off the Caribbean coast of Mexico

Books and magazines

You can find expert information on habitats in books and magazines in a library and study to become an expert yourself.

 Arctic Tundra (Earth's Last Frontiers) by Ellen Labrecque (Raintree)

 Subscribe to a magazine, such as Eco Kids Planet, www.ecokidsplanet.co.uk, to receive new information about animals and their habitats every month.

 www.animalfactguide.com

Umm al-Maa Lake, a Saharan Desert oasis in Libya

Museums and exhibitions

Paying a visit to a museum or an exhibition helps you to discover more about habitats around the world and the creatures that live in them.

 Life Cycles: Ocean by Sean Callery (Kingfisher)

 Horniman Museum, 100 London Road, Forest Hill, London SE23 3PQ

 www.kidsplanet.org/factsheets/map.html

The giraffe's home is on the savannah grasslands of Africa.

Documentaries and movies

Watching movies and documentaries is a great way to see how all kinds of creatures behave in their own environment.

 Africa (BBC Films)

 Enter into any creature's natural habitat without leaving your own home by searching for animal clips on the Internet.

www.bbc.co.uk/newsround/animals

OUR SOLAR
SYSTEM

THE SOLAR SYSTEM

The Sun's web of gravity stretches far out into space, and caught in that web are the planets, moons, rubble and dust that make up the Solar System. Everything in it moves continually around the Sun, with gravity and motion in perfect balance.

Building blocks

The inner planets are composed mainly of rock and metal, while the outer planets are mostly ice and gas. This is because when the Sun began to shine, the inner regions of the Solar System became so hot that only rock and metal worlds could survive there.

MERCURY
(first reached by
Mariner 10 *in 1974)*

Volume: 0.06 Earths
Mass: 0.06 Earths
Day length: 176 Earth-days
Year length: 88 Earth-days

EARTH
Volume: $1.09 \times 10^{12} km^3$
Mass: $5.98 \times 10^{24} kg$
Day length: 24h
Year length: 365.24 days

MARS
(first reached by
Mariner 4 *in 1965)*

Volume: 0.15 Earths
Mass: 0.11 Earths
Day length: 24h 37min
Year length: 687 Earth-days

VENUS
(first reached by
Mariner 2 *in 1962)*

Volume: 0.85 Earths
Mass: 0.82 Earths
Day length: 117 Earth-days
Year length: 225 Earth-days

JUPITER
(first reached by
Pioneer 10 *in 1973)*

Volume: 1,266 Earths
Mass: 318 Earths
Day length: 9h 55min
Year length: 12 Earth-years

Distances from the Sun

The planets closer to the Sun are also closer to each other. The Solar System began life as a cloud of dust and gas, and the Sun formed in its densest area. So the region nearest to our star had more materials with which to build planets.

Earth
150 million km

Venus
108 million km

Mars
228 million km

Jupiter
778 million km

SUN

Saturn
1,427 million km

Mercury
58 million km

 > Billions of years ago, there were dozens of planets in the Solar System.

If we were able to step outside the Solar System and look at it as a whole, the sunlit realm of the planets would be too tiny to see. Beyond the planets lies the ring-shaped Kuiper Belt, which is made up of icy objects. The Kuiper Belt merges into the Oort Cloud, an enormous area shaped like a hollow sphere, which contains the cores of comets. The whole Solar System is about two light-years across.

empty region

cross-section
of the Solar System

"We have swept through
all of the planets in the Solar
System, from Mercury to Neptune,
in a historic 20 [to] 30 year age
of spacecraft discovery."

Carl Sagan (1934–1996)
American astronomer and astrochemist

SATURN
(first reached by
Pioneer 11 *in 1979)*

Volume: 752 Earths
Mass: 95 Earths
Day length: 10h 39min
Year length: 29.5 Earth-years

NEPTUNE
(first reached by
Voyager 2 *in 1989)*

Volume: 59 Earths
Mass: 17 Earths
Day length: 16h 7min
Year length: 165 Earth-years

URANUS
(first reached by
Voyager 2 *in 1986)*

Volume: 64 Earths
Mass: 15 Earths
Day length: 17h 14min
Year length: 84 Earth-years

Uranus
2,871 million km

Neptune
4,497 million km

THE SUN

Our Sun is a vast ball of glowing gas, so large that a million Earths would fit inside it. Without its light and heat, there would be no life on Earth, and even our atmosphere would lie frozen solid on the ground. Although it is 150 million kilometres away, its light is still bright enough to damage our eyes. As the world spins around each day, the Sun moves across our skies.

Nuclear furnace

The Sun is made mostly of a light substance called hydrogen. Deep in its core, reactions like those in nuclear bombs convert the hydrogen into helium and release the enormous energy that we see as sunlight.

Light shows

The Sun sends out tiny particles, as well as light and heat. Near the north and south poles of Earth, these particles are caught in our planet's magnetic field, producing strange, coloured lights in the night sky. These spectacular displays are called aurorae.

Sun sailing

The Sun's light gently presses against everything it touches. Solar sails are light and shiny craft that drift through space, pushed by sunlight as sailing ships are pushed by wind.

Solar prominence

A prominence is a gigantic cloud of glowing gas – much larger than Earth – that floats in the Sun's atmosphere.

Sunspots are dark patches caused by the Sun's powerful magnetic field. They are darker than the rest of the Sun because they are cooler.

"One result of the evolution of our Sun... will very likely be the reduction of our Earth to a bleak, charred cinder."

Carl Sagan (1934–1996)
American astronomer and astrochemist

The temperature of the Sun's surface is about 5,500°C.

Solar eclipse

Every few months, the Moon passes directly between the Sun and Earth. When this happens, the Sun seems to turn black, and the glow of its corona appears around it. At other times, the corona is too dim to see against the Sun's bright light.

www.nasa.gov/vision/universe/solarsystem/sun_for_kids_main.html

MERCURY AND VENUS

Mercury and Venus are much closer to the Sun than
we are, which means they are much hotter than Earth.
They also move more quickly round the Sun than
we do, so their years are shorter than ours.

Colourful craters?

Like many photographs taken
in space, this *Mariner 10* image
has been falsely coloured to show
the different features more clearly.

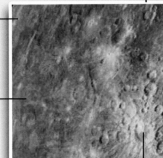

metal-rich area

solidified lava flow

Kuiper crater

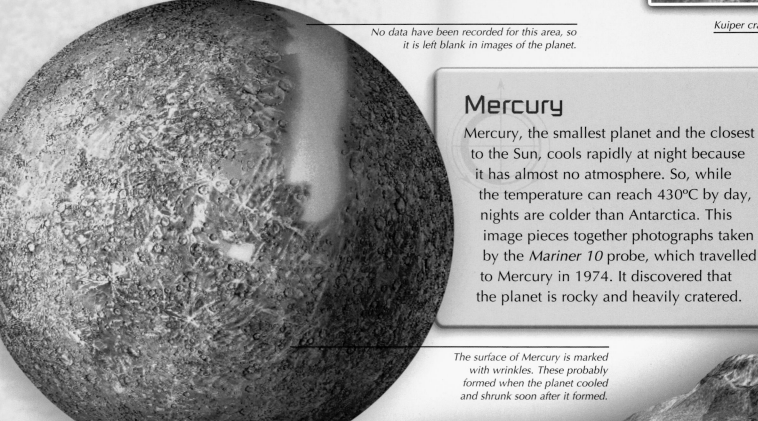

*No data have been recorded for this area, so
it is left blank in images of the planet.*

Mercury

Mercury, the smallest planet and the closest
to the Sun, cools rapidly at night because
it has almost no atmosphere. So, while
the temperature can reach 430ºC by day,
nights are colder than Antarctica. This
image pieces together photographs taken
by the *Mariner 10* probe, which travelled
to Mercury in 1974. It discovered that
the planet is rocky and heavily cratered.

*The surface of Mercury is marked
with wrinkles. These probably
formed when the planet cooled
and shrunk soon after it formed.*

> Although Mercury is much closer to the Sun than Venus, it is Venus that is the hotter planet.

Mapping Venus

The thick clouds of Venus always hide its surface from our telescopes. So, in 1989, the Magellan probe was sent to orbit the planet and map it by radar. It revealed that all of Venus's surface is young – only half a billion years old.

The Magellan probe orbited Venus for four years.

Maat Mons, the highest volcano on Venus

Lava domes

Many of the features that Magellan discovered on Venus are caused by volcanic activity. These domes are like nothing known on any other planet. They may have been caused by lava welling up under the ground, causing the surface to stretch and rise.

Only flashes of lightning brighten Venus's cloudy, dark surface.

Venus

Venus, our nearest neighbour, was once thought to be similar to Earth in prehistoric times. In fact, Venus is a deadly planet with an atmosphere as dense as a liquid. Rains of sulphuric acid fall from the cloudy, yellow sky, boiling away before reaching the ground. The greenhouse effect heats the planet's surface to 480ºC.

The 3-D maps of Venus produced by the Magellan probe show that most of its rocky surface is made up of smooth volcanic plains.

www.space.com/mercury and http://nssdc.gsfc.nasa.gov/photo_gallery/

EARTH

The distance of Earth from the Sun is what makes life on our planet possible. Living things need liquid water, and if we were much further from the Sun, all our water would be frozen as it is on Mars. If we were a little closer, water would boil as it would on Venus.

As the world is gradually heating up, our polar ice is melting. This causes flooding in low-lying areas.

Plants and trees produce oxygen, which all animals need to breathe. Plants also absorb the waste gases that animals breathe out.

Earth's atmosphere

An atmosphere is the layer of gases held around a planet by the force of its gravity. Earth's atmospheric gases keep the surface warm at night and protect it from dangerous Sun rays during the day. The atmosphere also helps to move water around. When water evaporates from the oceans, clouds form in the lowest layer of the atmosphere. The clouds bring rain to the land.

"We do not inherit the Earth from our ancestors, we borrow it from our children."

Haida Indian saying

 If all the ice on Earth melted, the seas would rise by 100m.

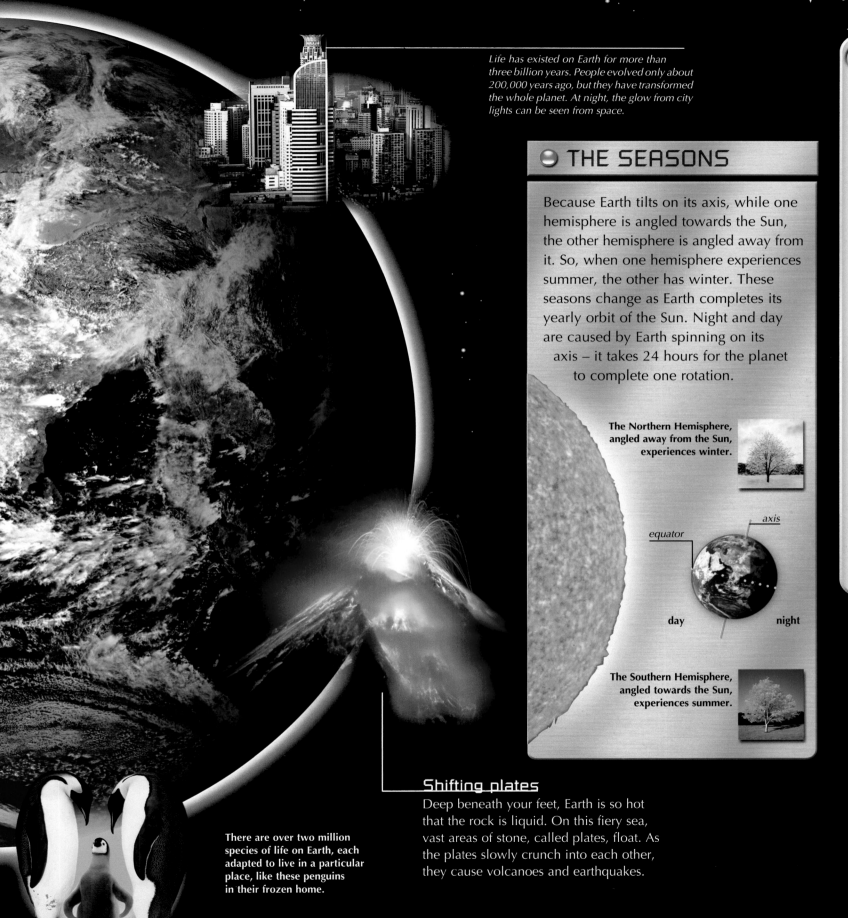

Life has existed on Earth for more than three billion years. People evolved only about 200,000 years ago, but they have transformed the whole planet. At night, the glow from city lights can be seen from space.

◉ THE SEASONS

Because Earth tilts on its axis, while one hemisphere is angled towards the Sun, the other hemisphere is angled away from it. So, when one hemisphere experiences summer, the other has winter. These seasons change as Earth completes its yearly orbit of the Sun. Night and day are caused by Earth spinning on its axis – it takes 24 hours for the planet to complete one rotation.

The Northern Hemisphere, angled away from the Sun, experiences winter.

axis

equator

day   night

The Southern Hemisphere, angled towards the Sun, experiences summer.

Shifting plates

Deep beneath your feet, Earth is so hot that the rock is liquid. On this fiery sea, vast areas of stone, called plates, float. As the plates slowly crunch into each other, they cause volcanoes and earthquakes.

There are over two million species of life on Earth, each adapted to live in a particular place, like these penguins in their frozen home.

MARS

Mars, the 'red planet', has fascinated people for more than a century. It is the second-closest planet to us and is the planet most like our own, with ice caps, seasons, volcanoes and deserts. In August 2012, NASA succeeded in landing a rover called *Curiosity* on Mars. *Curiosity* is investigating the possibility of life on Mars, and will provide much more data about the red planet than we have ever had before.

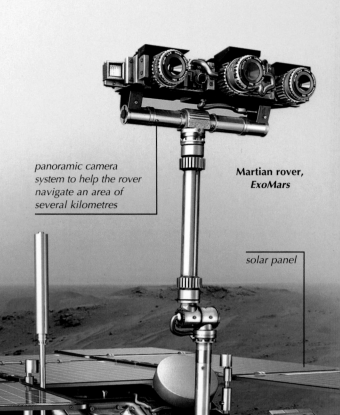

panoramic camera system to help the rover navigate an area of several kilometres

Martian rover, *ExoMars*

solar panel

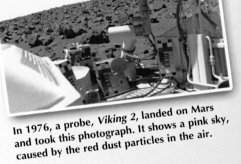

In 1976, a probe, *Viking 2*, landed on Mars and took this photograph. It shows a pink sky, caused by the red dust particles in the air.

ExoMars

The *ExoMars* rover is due to begin its exploration of the red planet in 2016 as part of a European Space Agency (ESA) project. The rover will be delivered by an orbiter, and will use balloons or parachutes to slow its descent and land safely. The rover will continue studies of the planet's rocks, building on *Viking 2*'s discovery that Martian soil is full of chemicals that would burn human skin.

six rugged wheels to cope with the planet's rocky terrain

 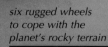 Mars is red because it is rusty. Long ago, iron in its desert soil combined with oxygen and painted the whole world red.

◉ ICE ON MARS

This bright-blue patch is a frozen pool of ice. It lies in a crater on Mars's vast northern plains. The photo was taken by ESA's *Mars Express Orbiter* in 2005. Although it was thought that water could not exist in liquid form on Mars because of the low atmospheric pressure, liquid water was discovered in 2015.

This instrument uses radar waves to 'see' up to 1km beneath the planet's surface.

antenna to communicate with Earth

solar panel to power orbiter

Mars Reconnaissance Orbiter

This spacecraft reached Mars in 2006 and it still circles the planet today. Its mission is to take pictures of the planet's surface, monitor the weather and study the rocks and ice. It is also looking for the best places for future spacecraft to land. One day, it will be used to pass messages from other missions back to Earth.

The frozen north

The *Reconnaissance Orbiter* took this photograph of Mars's northern polar region. It shows steep cliffs, almost 2km high, cloaked in ice.

Mars has permanently frozen ice at both its north and south poles. As on Earth, the ice caps grow or shrink according to the season.

"If [Mars rovers] find a rock that proves there was once life on Mars, it will be, without any doubt, the greatest scientific discovery ever made."

David McNab and James Younger
Writers and science-documentary producers

http://mars.jpl.nasa.gov

Jupiter's Great Red Spot is a giant hurricane – much larger than Earth – that has raged for centuries.

Ganymede,
the largest moon
in the Solar System, is
bigger than Mercury.

Callisto
is made largely
of ice.

Io
is sprinkled
with erupting
volcanoes.

Europa
has liquid seas
under its icy crust.

JUPITER
AND SATURN

Jupiter and Saturn are gas giants – huge worlds with deep atmospheres concealing cores of rock and ice. Both have rings – Jupiter's are faint dust belts, whereas Saturn's rings are made of rocky ice – and both have at least 60 moons each. The planets spin so fast that they have very short days and the flattened-sphere shape of a grapefruit. Both are still cooling from their formation, and this leftover heat generates storms that never end.

Many moons

Jupiter has at least 63 moons, many of them locked by gravity so that one side always faces the planet. Some, like Io, are warmed by the stretching and squeezing effects of Jupiter's gravity. Others crumble into space, their dust forming rings round the planet.

CORE – *the central part of a planet*

Jupiter is large enough to contain all the other planets.

Jupiter

Jupiter is the giant planet of our Solar System, more massive than all the others combined. Although it is more than four times as far from us as the Sun, it can be the brightest object in the night sky. Jupiter is surrounded by a zone of deadly radiation and an enormous magnetic field.

www.esa.int/esaKIDSen/OurUniverse.html

Light world

Although Saturn weighs more than 95 times the weight of Earth, it is still the lightest planet for its size in the Solar System. It is so light that it would float in water.

Saturn's rings are shown in false colour here. The pink rings contain only large rocks; green and blue include smaller fragments as well.

Saturn

Saturn's ring system is composed of billions of orbiting fragments of icy rock that range in size from dust particles to boulders. They may be the remains of a moon-sized object that strayed too close to Saturn and was torn apart by the planet's gravity.

ORBIT – the path of one object around another in space

URANUS AND NEPTUNE

The two outermost planets of our Solar System, Uranus and Neptune, are gas giants like Jupiter and Saturn. Far out in space, the Sun shines dimly, so these worlds are cold and dark. As they move slowly around the Sun on huge orbits, they have long years – Uranus's year is 84 Earth-years long and Neptune's is 165.

Uranus

Uranus was discovered in 1781 by English astronomer William Herschel (1738–1822), and reached by space probe 197 years later. This giant planet, circled by dark rings of black boulders, gets its green colour from the methane in its atmosphere. Uranus spins on its back, probably knocked over by a collision with a wandering planet billions of years ago.

Miranda, a moon of Uranus

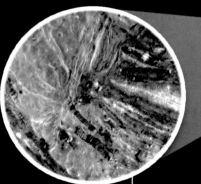

Miranda's surface is so jumbled that some scientists think the moon was shattered long ago and then reassembled when gravity pulled the fragments together again.

 On some parts of Uranus, night can last for more than 40 Earth-years.

Voyages to remote worlds

The twin Voyager space probes, *Voyager 1* and *Voyager 2*, explored the outer planets in the 1970s and 1980s. Both probes will travel beyond the Solar System for many thousands of years – although they will cease to function in the 2020s. In about 40,000 years, *Voyager 2* will reach a nearby star.

instruments to record energy and light data

Generators provide electrical power.

antenna dish

A magnometer on the arm measures magnetic forces.

Voyager 2 used the gravity of Uranus to propel itself towards Neptune.

Vast white clouds of methane ice rush across a dark storm system on the face of Neptune, the windiest planet in the Solar System.

"I saw, O, first of all mankind,
I saw the disk of my new planet gliding there
beyond our tumults, in that realm of peace."

Herschel's discovery of Uranus
From Alfred Noyes's poem The Torch-Bearers, 1937

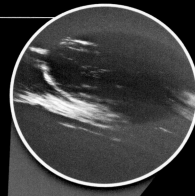

http://photojournal.jpl.nasa.gov/index.html

Neptune

The colour of the outermost planet in our Solar System gives it its name – Neptune, god of the blue sea. Unlike the other giants, some of Neptune's rings are incomplete arcs. This cold planet generates some heat of its own and this powers its dramatic weather systems. However, its largest moon, Triton, may be the coldest moon in the Solar System.

Nitrogen, which makes up most of our air, is mainly frozen solid on Neptune's moon Triton. However, sometimes it squirts upwards as liquid jets, before being knocked sideways by high-altitude winds.

INVESTIGATE

Scientists know more about our Solar System than ever before and you can use books, websites and visitor attractions to learn how they made their discoveries.

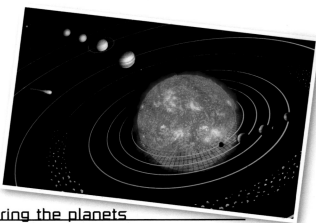

the planets of our Solar System as they orbit the Sun

Exploring the planets

You can explore the planets in our Solar System by exploring the Internet to find not only fascinating websites, but also some brilliant visitor attractions.

 13 Planets: The Latest View of the Solar System by David A. Aguilar (National Geographic Kids)

 Morrison Planetarium, California Academy of Sciences, 55 Music Concourse Dr, San Francisco, CA 94118, United States

 www.nasa.gov

NASA's *ExoMars* rover is designed to explore the Red Planet.

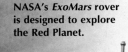

Books and magazines

Most science-based visitor attractions have book shops or libraries where you can read more about the planets.

 It's All About: Super Solar System (Kingfisher)

 Planetarium, Explore-At-Bristol, Anchor Road, Harbourside, Bristol BS1 5DB

Saturn is famous for its rings of ice, dust and rock debris.

 **www.skyatnightmagazine.com**

Museums and exhibitions

A visit to a science or space museum will show you how astronauts and space probes have explored space.

 The Kingfisher Space Encyclopedia (Kingfisher)

 Science Museum, Exhibition Road, London SW7 2DD

Earth sunrise, as seen from space

 www.spacecentre.co.uk/tour/sir-patrick-moore-planetarium

Documentaries and movies

Take a closer look at the Solar System by watching film footage recorded by astronauts or probes. Science-fiction films can also fire your imagination about other worlds and alien life!

 https://www.nasa.gov/multimedia/hd/apollo11_hdpage.html

 IMAX 3D cinema, Science Museum, Exhibition Road, South Kensington, London SW7 2DD

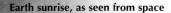 **www.bbc.co.uk/science/space**

A SKY
OF STARS

STAR-GAZING

STAR - a giant ball of gas that generates heat and light

For thousands of years, people have gazed at the starlit sky and asked questions. And for centuries, telescopes have shown them the answers – and raised more questions. When trying to understand strange planets and distant stars, scientists use images sent by telescopes, both those on Earth and those that drift through space high above us.

Observatory

In the desert of Arizona, USA, Kitt Peak National Observatory is home to 19 optical telescopes. The telescopes use huge mirrors to gather light from stars and form images of them.

Solar panels convert sunlight into electricity to power the Hubble.

Radio telescope

There are many types of light that we cannot see but special telescopes can. This one, in Hawaii, picks up radio waves from the stars. The photograph took many minutes to make. During that time, the stars appeared to circle in the sky as Earth spun on its axis.

Hubble Space Telescope

Many of our best photographs of space are produced by this optical telescope. The Hubble has been in orbit since 1990, when it travelled into space onboard a space shuttle. It produces much clearer images than Earth-based telescopes can. The motion of air in Earth's atmosphere blurs images (causing stars to appear to twinkle). Floating beyond our atmosphere, the Hubble does not have this problem.

The 'forward shell' houses the primary mirror, which collects light and reflects it towards a secondary mirror. This mirror focuses the light onto detectors to create an image.

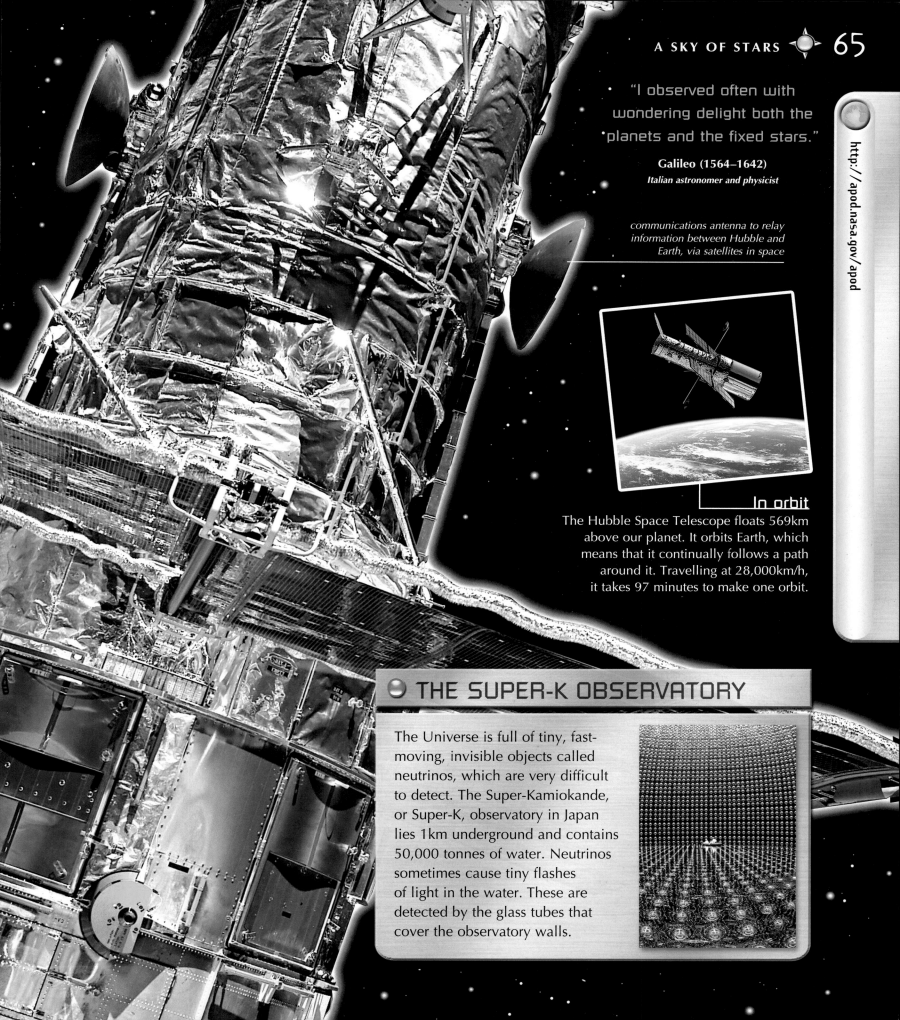

"I observed often with
wondering delight both the
planets and the fixed stars."

Galileo (1564–1642)
Italian astronomer and physicist

http://apod.nasa.gov/apod

*communications antenna to relay
information between Hubble and
Earth, via satellites in space*

In orbit

The Hubble Space Telescope floats 569km
above our planet. It orbits Earth, which
means that it continually follows a path
around it. Travelling at 28,000km/h,
it takes 97 minutes to make one orbit.

◉ THE SUPER-K OBSERVATORY

The Universe is full of tiny, fast-
moving, invisible objects called
neutrinos, which are very difficult
to detect. The Super-Kamiokande,
or Super-K, observatory in Japan
lies 1km underground and contains
50,000 tonnes of water. Neutrinos
sometimes cause tiny flashes
of light in the water. These are
detected by the glass tubes that
cover the observatory walls.

THE UNIVERSE

About 13.7 billion years ago, the Universe began – time, space and energy appeared, and space expanded rapidly. That expansion, and the fading flash of the beginning of everything, still continues today.

When the Universe was cool enough, tiny particles of matter and antimatter formed. By the end of the first second, most of these particles had destroyed each other.

The matter that remained was not spread evenly through space. Gradually, the gravity of the denser areas attracted more matter, further increasing their density. Galaxies would later form in these areas, which are shown below in blue.

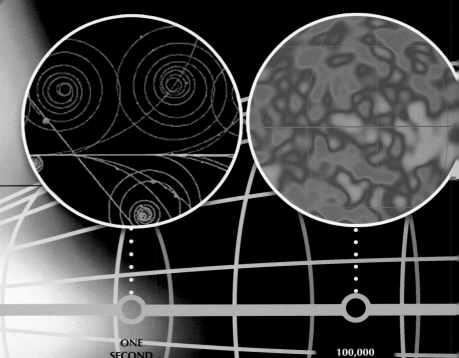

electrons and anti-electrons created in a laboratory (this happened naturally in the early Universe)

The cause of the Big Bang is science's greatest unsolved mystery.

The Universe underwent a sudden jump in the rate of its expansion.

ZERO TIME

LESS THAN ONE TRILLIONTH OF A SECOND

ONE SECOND

100,000 YEARS

Dark matter and dark energy

Most of the Universe is invisible because every galaxy is loaded with dark matter, which may consist of particles of an unknown type. The whole of space is filled with dark energy, a mysterious force that opposes the pull of gravity.

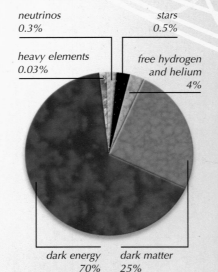

The blue glow is dark matter; the pink area is ordinary matter.

The composition of the Universe

neutrinos 0.3%

stars 0.5%

heavy elements 0.03%

free hydrogen and helium 4%

dark energy 70%

dark matter 25%

"The size and age of the cosmos are beyond ordinary human understanding. Lost somewhere between immensity and eternity is our tiny planetary home."

Carl Sagan (1934–1996)
American astronomer and astrochemist

> The Sun is about one third of the age of the Universe.

When the Universe had cooled to about 3,000°C, atoms (mostly hydrogen) formed from smaller particles. Only then could light shine through space.

The first generation of stars formed from hydrogen and helium. During their lives, they built up heavier elements and when they died – as supernovae – those elements were scattered through space. The picture below shows how the formation of the first star may have looked.

The heavy elements from the first stars form part of the Sun and the other stars that exist today. The temperature of the Universe today has fallen, after billions of years, to –270°C.

www.bbc.co.uk/science/space/universe/questions_and_ideas/big_bang

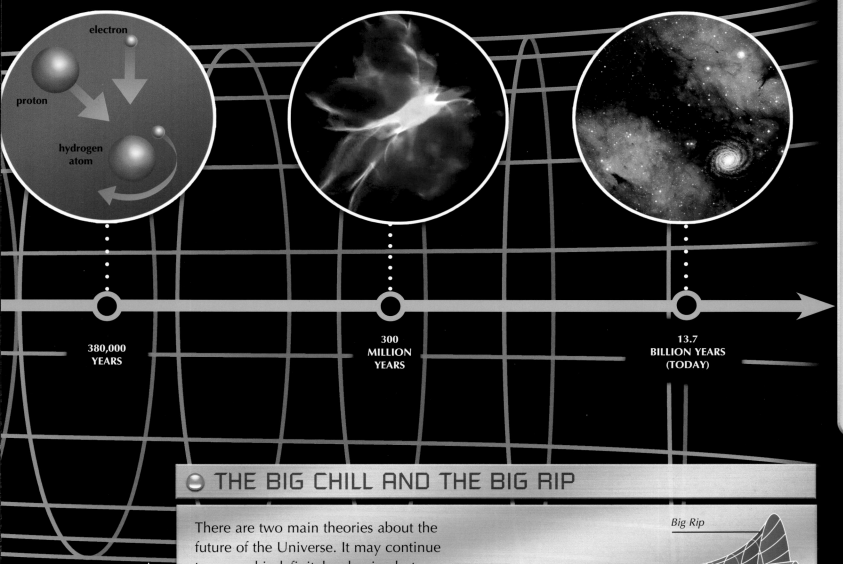

electron

proton

hydrogen atom

380,000 YEARS

300 MILLION YEARS

13.7 BILLION YEARS (TODAY)

The early Universe changed very rapidly, and then the pace of change slowed, so this timeline of key events is not to scale.

◉ THE BIG CHILL AND THE BIG RIP

There are two main theories about the future of the Universe. It may continue to expand indefinitely, slowing but never stopping. All the stars would burn out until everything became dark and cold – a Big Chill. However, there are signs and theories that the rate of the Universe's expansion is increasing. One day, galaxies, stars, planets and atoms may all tear themselves apart – a Big Rip.

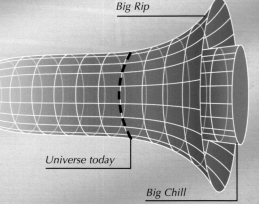

Big Rip

Big Bang

Universe today

Big Chill

GALAXIES

GALAXY - a collection of stars, gas, dust and dark matter

Stars are not spread evenly throughout the Universe – they are grouped into galaxies, each one containing millions, billions or trillions of stars. Many galaxies are like gigantic whirlpools of stars, while others are more like discs, or balls, or softly glowing clouds of light.

New stars are born in the spiral arms of this galaxy.

A dwarf galaxy

No one knows for sure how galaxies form, but it may be that they begin life like this young galaxy, which is much smaller than our own. The red glow in the centre is the light of ancient stars, while young new ones burn blue in the outer regions.

The Whirlpool Galaxy

In spiral galaxies like this, the curving arms, which are marked by lanes of thick black dust, are regions of starbirth. Like most other galaxies, the Whirlpool Galaxy is rushing away from us as the Universe expands and the distances between galaxies grow. Every second, the galaxy is 500km further away.

Andromeda spiral

This galaxy is the most distant thing we can see with the naked eye. It is a trillion times brighter than the Sun, but so far away (2.5 million light-years) that it can be seen only on the darkest of nights.

 > Billions of years ago, most galaxies were blue due to the large number of stars forming in them.

This fuzzy glow is a small galaxy passing close to the Whirlpool Galaxy. Its gravity may be triggering starbirth in the Whirlpool's arms.

Galaxies shine with both visible and invisible radiation. This photograph shows not just visible light but also ultraviolet radiation from new stars in the outer ring and heat radiation from older stars in the core.

⊖ OUR GALAXY – THE MILKY WAY

Our Sun and the Solar System lie in one of the Milky Way's outer arms.

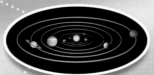

The milky stripe of light in our night sky is our own galaxy, the Milky Way, seen from the inside. The galaxy contains billions of stars, and orbiting some of them are planets that may be similar to those in our own Solar System.

From the side, the galaxy would look flat, with the yellow nucleus of older stars bulging at its centre.

The Milky Way appears brighter from the Southern Hemisphere, as the South Pole points roughly towards the bright galactic core.

SPACE CLOUDS

GAS – a state of matter in which a substance expands to fill its container

When people started to study the night sky with telescopes, they found fuzzy patches, which they called nebulae, meaning clouds. Many of these nebulae really are clouds – of glowing or dark dust or gas. They are places of starbirth or star death. Other nebulae are nearby clusters of stars, and some are distant galaxies.

Pillars of Creation

In these vast columns of dust and gas, which form part of the Eagle Nebula, new stars are being born. Powerful radiation from hot young stars nearby heats the outer layers of the columns to form the bluish green mist that can be seen around them.

Starbirth

This telescope image shows a wider view of the Eagle Nebula with an exploding star at its glowing core. Exploding stars (supernovae) squeeze parts of surrounding cloud, creating dense regions. Gravity continues the process, and the squeezed regions get more and more dense. They also get hotter – their centres get so hot that nuclear reactions begin, turning these central areas into stars.

Small protusion contain globules dense gas that a the beginning of new star.

> Many of the atoms we are made of spent millions of years in a molecular cloud after forming in an exploding star.

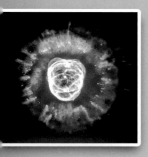

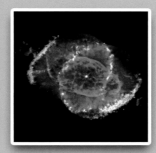

http://hubblesite.org/gallery/album/nebula

At only 1,000 years old, the Eskimo Nebula is very young. Astronomer William Herschel discovered it in 1787. Later, he described spherical nebulae like the Eskimo as 'planetary nebulae'.

A planetary nebula, which is gas thrown off by a star, is usually sphere-shaped. The Cat's Eye Nebula, however, has a much more complex shape. No one is sure why.

The Crab Nebula is the remains of a supernova – a massive star exploding at the end of its life. The light from the explosion reached Earth in 1054.

The Orion Nebula is the easiest to see from Earth. This detail shows the Horsehead, a dark cloud of dust silhouetted against the glow of a hot gas cloud called an emission nebula.

Each Pillar is about one light-year long. This means that it would take light one year to travel from the top to the bottom.

"...the nebulae [are] amazing us by the strangeness of their forms and the incomprehensibility of their nature..."

Mary Somerville (1780–1872)
Scottish science writer

The Pillars may no longer exist – a nearby supernova explosion might have destroyed them 6,000 years ago. If so, we will not see that destruction for a thousand years as the Pillars are 7,000 light-years away.

BRIGHT DUST SHELLS

Many ageing stars throw off shells of dust, and many others flash and pulse with light. These images show both: the central star has sent a burst of light that is spreading gradually through the dust shells, lighting up one after another.

The red glow at the centre of the dust shells is a supergiant star.

The black regions are holes in the dust shells.

The outermost dust shell is about the size of Jupiter.

Blue giant

A blue giant, a thousand times larger than the Sun, is as hot as a star can be without destroying itself. Its vast power boils away its atmosphere and floods the region around it with harsh blue light and deadly radiation.

STRANGE STARS

The Sun is a very ordinary star that has changed little in temperature or brightness during the history of life on Earth. This is lucky for us – if it had changed much, we would probably not be here to see it. But many other stars are strange – they pulsate, change shape, join together or blow apart. And while some are incredibly hot, others barely smoulder.

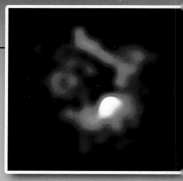

Carbon star

Some cool, red stars have atmospheres rich in carbon, which condenses around them in the form of sooty clouds. The clouds filter the light of their parent star, making its glow an even deeper red.

Distorted star

Not all stars are round. Mira (from the Latin for 'wonderful') looks distorted. This is either because it changes shape as it pulsates or because some of its surface is too dark to see.

PULSATE – grow regularly larger and smaller

Contact binaries

Binary stars – a pair of stars that orbit each other – are very common. However, it is rare to find any that are so close that they touch, like these pictured here. Stars that do touch each other, share each other's atmospheres and distort each other's shapes.

www.aavso.org/variable-stars-main

Variables and demons

When stars change in brightness, they are called variables. Some variable stars suddenly flash with light or are darkened by clouds of dust. Other stars brighten and dim regularly. This may be caused by other, dimmer stars orbiting them and blocking their light. The first such star to be discovered is called Algol, from the Arabic word for 'demon'.

The brown dwarf is bound by gravity to this bigger and brighter red dwarf.

Brown dwarf

Brown dwarfs are dim objects, heavier than planets but lighter than true stars. Strangely, although their masses range from 20 to 80 times that of Jupiter, they are all about the same size.

"Classifying the stars has helped materially in all studies of the structure of the Universe..."

Annie Jump Cannon (1863–1941)
American astronomer

● PULSATING STARS

Astronomers can work out the average true brightnesses of Cepheid stars, which are pulsating stars, from the times they take to fade and brighten. Taking into account the fact that all stars look dimmer the further away they are, the scientists can then work out the stars' distances from Earth.

A pulsating star is hottest and brightest when it is small.

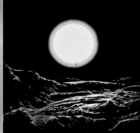

As the star swells, it fades, cools and reddens.

Some stars take only a few hours to swell and shrink; others take several years.

DEATH

Stars are like factories, converting hydrogen to helium, and helium to other elements, and producing floods of energy to light our skies by day and night. This nuclear-processing may continue steadily for billions of years. However, eventually, further conversion of elements becomes impossible, and stars die. But they don't go quietly...

When there is no fuel left to burn, the outer layers of a red giant swell, forming a bubble-like 'planetary nebula' (which has nothing to do with planets).

The nebula is made of such thin gas that its core – a white dwarf – can be seen. The white dwarf, which will take billions of years to cool, is the final stage in the life of medium and small-sized stars.

The Hourglass Nebula was probably shaped by wind expansion in a cloud that was more dense at its poles than at its equator.

When the hydrogen fuel in the core of stars with a similar mass to the Sun runs out, nuclear reactions in outer layers take over. This causes the star to swell and cool, turning it into a red giant.

Stars burn for millions or billions of years – the more massive they are, the more quickly they burn up and the shorter their lives.

Two paths to death

What happens when a star dies depends on its mass. Stars like the Sun swell enormously, melting and engulfing their closest planets (see path from left to above). More massive stars die in supernova explosions brighter than galaxies (see path from left, down then right). Supernovae can both trigger the birth of new stars and provide the building materials for them.

When they run out of hydrogen, massive stars swell up into supergiants – perhaps a million times the volume of the Sun and a hundred thousand times brighter. Many supergiants are pulsating variables, brightening as they shrink and fading as they swell.

 > The first pulsar was labelled LGM-1 – 'Little Green Men' – as some thought its signal was an alien message.

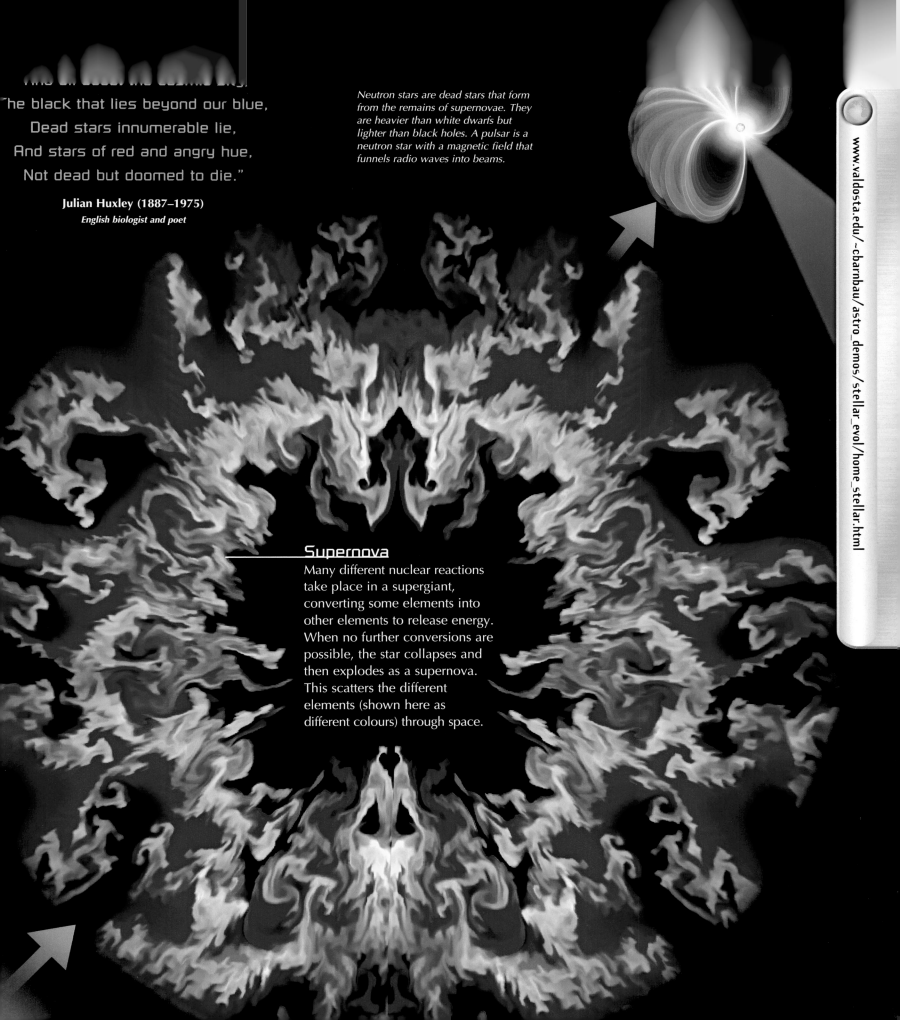

"…he black that lies beyond our blue,
 Dead stars innumerable lie,
 And stars of red and angry hue,
 Not dead but doomed to die."

Julian Huxley (1887–1975)
English biologist and poet

*Neutron stars are dead stars that form
from the remains of supernovae. They
are heavier than white dwarfs but
lighter than black holes. A pulsar is a
neutron star with a magnetic field that
funnels radio waves into beams.*

www.valdosta.edu/~cbarnbau/astro_demos/stellar_evol/home_stellar.html

Supernova

Many different nuclear reactions
take place in a supergiant,
converting some elements into
other elements to release energy.
When no further conversions are
possible, the star collapses and
then explodes as a supernova.
This scatters the different
elements (shown here as
different colours) through space.

INVESTIGATE

Reach for the stars by discovering more about the
Universe in museums, at exhibitions or observatories,
in books or on the Internet.

Stargazing

You can become an astronomer quite easily just by looking up at the night sky.
Stars, planets, satellites and galaxies can all be seen with the naked eye.

Andromeda is the nearest galaxy to ours.

the Griffith Observatory in Los Angeles, California, United States

 Basher Science: Astronomy by Dan Green (Kingfisher)

 Greenwich Royal Observatory, National Maritime Museum, London SE10 9NF

www.schoolsobservatory.org.uk

Books and magazines

Find out what stars and galaxies you can see from where you live
by doing a little research in a library.

 Stars and Constellations by Dr Raman K Prinja (Heinemann)

 Planetarium, Explore-At-Bristol, Anchor Road, Harbourside, Bristol BS1 5DB

http://spaceplace.nasa.gov/starfinder/en/

Observatories and exhibitions

Use the Internet to search for an observatory near you that you can visit
or ask at local museums about astronomy and space exhibitions.

 The Sun by Michael Carlowicz and Steele Hill (Harry N. Abrams)

 Sydney Observatory, 1003 Upper Fort St, Millers Point, NSW, 2000, Australia

the Hubble Space Telescope in orbit around the Earth

http://www.jodrellbank.net

Stars are fuel by hydrogen.

Documentaries and movies

Take a trip into outer space with amazing documentaries and films that will show
you other worlds, without you even leaving home!

 Stephen Hawking's Universe (Discovery Channel DVD)

 www.youtube.com/watch?v=zR3Igc3Rhfg

www.space.com/57-stars-formation-classification-and-constellations.html

GLOSSARY

algae
A group of plant species that ranges from simple, single-celled organisms to various sea weeds and even giant kelp.

anemone
A flowering plant on land, but in the sea an anemone is an animal similar to coral. The sea anemone is named after the flowering plant.

antenna
A radio antenna, or aerial, is a device that sends or receives radio signals.

atmosphere
Layer of gases around a star, planet or moon.

atom
The smallest part of an element, composed of a nucleus made of protons and neutrons. Electrons are arranged around the nucleus.

axis
An imaginary line that passes through the poles of a planet and on which a planet spins.

bromeliad
A family of plants that includes flowering plants, mosses and the pineapple.

coniferous
Trees and shrubs that produce seeds in cones. Most do not shed their leaves in autumn.

cosmos
Another word for the Universe.

deciduous
Trees and shrubs that shed their leaves each year in autumn.

element
A substance made of atoms that all have the same number of protons.

energy
Energy is what is required for work to be done, such as lifting an object. There are many types of energy, including sound, light, heat, electricity and mass.

fissure
A narrow crack or split in earth or rock.

galaxy
A large number of stars, planets, gas, dust and dark matter, which are held together by gravity.

gravity
A force of attraction between objects.

greenhouse effect
The rising temperature in the atmosphere caused by the build-up of carbon dioxide, methane and other gases.

helium
A very light substance, which is a gas at all but the lowest temperatures.

hemisphere
Half of a sphere.

hydrogen
A very light substance, the most common in the Universe. Most stars are made mainly of hydrogen.

iron
One of the most common elements on Earth. Iron forms a large part of Earth's outer and inner cores as well as the Earth's crust.

Kuiper Belt
Lumps of ice and other frozen material in orbit beyond Neptune.

laccolith
An underground layer of rock or magma that pushes other layers upwards to form a domed shape on the surface.

magnetic field
An area surrounding a moving electric charge or a magnet that pushes and pulls on other magnets, charges and objects.

mammal
A warm-blooded animal that feeds its young on the mother's milk.

mass
A measure of the amount of matter in an object. In a gravitational field, the more mass an object has, the heavier it is.

matter
Substance that has mass and takes up space. Matter exists in four main forms: solid, liquid, gas and plasma.

meteor
A shooting star caused by a space rock burning up in our atmosphere. If part of the rock reaches the ground it is called a meteorite.

methane
A colourless gas that is made up of carbon and hydrogen.

moon
A large, rocky sphere that travels round a planet in orbit.

nebula (plural: nebulae)
A cloud of dust and gas in space.

neutrino
A particle smaller than an atom, which exists in enormous numbers. They can pass through almost everything – even the Earth – without stopping. Neutrinos are very difficult to detect.

neutron
A neutron is a particle found in the nucleus of every atom except for hydrogen. A neutron star is a dead star in which the gravity is so high that its protons and electrons are crushed together and turn into neutrons.

nitrogen
A colourless, odourless gas that is one of the most common elements in the universe. Nitrogen makes up 78 per cent of the Earth's atmosphere.

nuclear
Nuclear means 'relating to the nucleus of an atom'. Nuclear fusion is the process in which hydrogen is converted to helium in the Sun, releasing the energy we see as sunlight and starlight.

nucleus (plural: nuclei)
The core of an atom.

oasis
A fertile area of desert where surface water can be found.

orbit
The path of one object around another in space, such as a planet around a star.

orbiter
A spacecraft that is designed to orbit a planet. It may send probes to the surface, but never lands itself.

Pangaea
A supercontinent believed to have existed when all of the Earth's other land masses were joined together over 200 million years ago.

panorama
An unbroken view of the surrounding scenery. A panoramic camera can provide photographs through 360°.

Panthalassa
A single ocean that may have surrounded the Pangaea land mass.

particle
A tiny fragment of matter.

prehistoric
Describes a period in time before humans began to compile records of events.

probe
An uncrewed spaceship sent to explore other worlds and gather information that it sends back to scientists on Earth.

proton
A particle with a positive electric charge found in the nuclei of all atoms.

radar
A system in which radio waves are beamed towards objects and are bounced back. Radar is used to track moving objects, map the surfaces of planets and to measure their distances from the Earth.

radiation
A form of energy that travels through space as electromagnetic waves. Light, radio, infrared, ultraviolet, X-rays and gamma rays are all types of radiation.

radio
A form of electromagnetic radiation, with waves much longer than light waves.

red dwarf
The most common type of star in the Milky Way. They are smaller than the Sun and do not burn as brightly.

reptile
A cold-blooded animal such as a snake or lizard that has dry, scaly skin and lays soft-shelled eggs.

Richter Scale
A method of measuring the movement of the ground, especially during earthquakes. It was developed by American Charles Richter in the 1930s.

satellite
An object in orbit around a planet. A moon is a natural satellite; a weather satellite is an artificial one.

solar panel
Solar means 'relating to the Sun'. A solar panel is a device that converts sunlight into heat or electricity.

sonar
A device for locating objects. Sonar is similar to radar but uses sound waves instead of radio waves.

species
A group of plants or animals that are of a similar type.

star
A glowing mass of gas, held together by gravity.

sulphuric acid
A strong, colourless acid that can burn the skin and dissolve metal.

supernova
A type of exploding star.

temperate
A temperate region is an area far enough from the equator and from the poles to have mild temperatures.

tropical
Regions close to the equator where the environment is hot and humid.

vapour
Gas or tiny drops of liquid that can be suspended in the air like mist.

volume
A measure of the amount of space that something occupies.

white dwarf
The hot, bright core of a small or medium-sized star in the final stages of its existence.

INDEX